Prai

BE NOT AFR

"A radical and revolutionary act of love, transcendently written. Mimi Zhu writes about love in a way that is tender and caring and healing—they contextualize love not as an abstract sentiment but as a grounded and spiritual act intimately tied to every aspect of what we fight for."

—Jonny Sun, *New York Times* bestselling author of *Goodbye, Again*

"Tender, insightful, and deeply affirming. These precious chapters are a nourishing constellation of hope, truths, new light, and the words on love and fellowship that we need, have always needed."

—Yrsa Daley-Ward, poet and author of *bone*, *The Terrible*, and *The How*

"Zhu conveys their story with such honesty and clarity that it forges connections to your heart straight through the page. With incredible strength they lay out not only the darkness of their experiences with assault but also their path to love, to full acceptance of their past, of their emotions, and, in the end, themself. *Be Not Afraid of Love* brings forward wisdom teachings like impermanence and the law of karma in a way that is accessible and relatable to a new generation. This book is bound to help those who are ready to reclaim their power."

—Yung Pueblo, *New York Times* bestselling author of *Clarity & Connection*

PENGUIN LIFE

BE NOT AFRAID OF LOVE

Mimi Zhu (they/them) is a queer Chinese Australian writer and artist. They facilitate workshops that are dedicated to the healing power of the written word. Their work has been featured in *The New York Times, PAPER, i-D, The Guardian, Printed Matter, VICE,* and more. They are based in Brooklyn.

@mimizhuxiyuan

BE NOT AFRAID
OF LOVE

Lessons on Fear, Intimacy,
and Connection

Mimi Zhu

life

PENGUIN BOOKS

An imprint of Penguin Random House LLC
penguinrandomhouse.com

A Penguin Life Book

Artwork by Somnath Bhatt

LIBRARY OF CONGRESS CATALOGING-IN-PUBLICATION DATA

Names: Zhu, Mimi, author.
Title: Be not afraid of love: lessons on fear,
intimacy, and connection /
Mimi Zhu.
Description: First Edition. | New York:
Penguin Life, [2022] | Includes
bibliographical references.
Identifiers: LCCN 2022002725 (print) |
LCCN 2022002726 (ebook) |
ISBN 9780143137122 (trade paperback) |
ISBN 9780593511091 (ebook)
Subjects: LCSH: Love. | Fear. | Intimacy (Psychology) |
Interpersonal relations.
Classification: LCC BF575.L8 Z48 2022 (print) |
LCC BF575.L8 (ebook) |
DDC 152.4/1—dc23/eng/20220608
LC record available at https://lccn.loc.gov/2022002725
LC ebook record available at https://lccn.loc.gov/2022002726

Printed in the United States of America
5th Printing

Set in Weiss
Designed by Sabrina Bowers

For my families: biological, chosen, and of Earth.
You have all shown me what it means to be embodiments of love.

Contents

Preface

I must be honest; I am terrified of love.

I cannot act as an authority on the mystery that is love, for I have spent a long time cowering from it, fearful of it, and avoiding it at all costs. As much as I have tried running away from it, I have learned that love is an inescapable force, and my entire life revolves around its power. Maybe it is not love that I am afraid of, but the loss, heartbreak, vulnerability, and death that come with it. I write to uncover all the possibilities that live, breathe, and await me underneath my fear. In this book, I share with you my humble findings, which is my act of love to anybody who will receive it, and an act of love toward myself.

Since my childhood, I have been curious about the visceral natures of both love and fear. I have been enthralled by the giddiness of love and stung by the prickliness of fear. I have seen how often they meet during grief, intimacy, anxiety, post-traumatic stress disorder, romance, friendship, and communion. Love and fear create myriad emotions and projections in our internal emotional landscapes, and they also echo outward to generate relationships, community, history, political movements, and violence in the world we live in. Love and fear are not one and the same, but they exist on a spectrum that invites them to be intertwined in a rapturous hypnotic dance.

I am a survivor of intimate partner violence. For a little over three years, I was deeply entangled in an abusive, toxic, on-again, off-again relationship. We went through painful cycles of fear and love, and had a difficult time differentiating between the two. The relationship was addictive and violent, and by the time it ended, I felt as if I had lost myself completely. I searched everywhere for answers because I still believed that love lived outside me, far beyond my grasp. It took me years to realize that love has a home in me. I needed to embody love to truly understand it.

The last five years have been an ongoing urgent quest of healing, and it continues without any specific destination in mind. I have spent most of my life escaping my pain and seeking refuge in different people and places. In doing so, I have witnessed love in many unexpected forms. On some days my fear overcomes me, and I do not believe in the power of love, but on most days, I experience embodied moments when I wholeheartedly feel love's endurance, love's patience, and love's will for me to survive. Writing this book has helped me live, and living this life has helped me write. I hope to share these moments with you, in hopes that my love finds yours.

I wish to acknowledge and honor my limitations. My writing comes from personal experiences in childhood and adulthood, and I am not taking a stance as an authority on feeling. I commit to speaking of my experiences from the "I"; the "I" who is interconnected with you in precious and different ways. I will not tell anybody what to do, or how to feel their feelings, and I am hopeful that my offerings will resonate with whoever might need them.

I wish to emphasize that I cannot speak for all survivors of intimate violence. Abolitionist and writer K Agbebiyi wrote, "Survivors are not a monolith" in an Instagram post that I return to often.* Survivors have different and nuanced needs for healing and grieving. I speak about my own personal experiences and the changes I wish to see in varying kinds of survivor-centered support.

Neema Githere, a theorist and a close friend, taught me that we must all engage in *vigorous citation practices*,† and I must acknowledge that much of my writing comes from being in conversation with people in my communities. I could not possibly have written this book without being in active conversation with friends, chosen family, community members, and collectives, and I commit to citing and referencing the people whom I am fortunate enough to know, love, and admire. I acknowledge that there is a lot that I do not know, and that I live in the vast space of perpetual knowing, unknowing, learning, and unlearning.

I am an able-bodied Australian-born queer Chinese femme person who grew up in lower-middle-class backgrounds in Australia and Singapore. I did not grow up with access to wealth, and my family's financial status was constantly fluctuating. However, I did have consistent access to housing and food. I am not a licensed therapist, nor do I have a formal education in psychology or social work. I am a survivor of intimate violence and abuse, and I write my own story. It is my responsibility to be honest about my identity as well as my privileges. I want to also acknowledge that the primary abusive relationship that I will be unpacking in this book was with a queer non-white cisgender man. I mention this to say

---

*You can read the post at instagram.com/p/CMMwK2hlrR4/.

†You can read more of Neema's ingenious work at their website, presentism 2020.com.

that in public our relationship benefited from heteronormative privileges, and in private the violence within our dynamic forced me to see how patriarchal violence can destroy relationships, enact power-over domination, and cause irreversible harm.

Many of my reflections are derived from Buddhist teachings. I practice Buddhism by learning from my ancestors and sangha (community) and reading, meditating, and attending ceremonies. Buddhism taught me that as a survivor I could not escape my suffering in order to heal from it. To access my full loving being, I needed to sit with my suffering. While Buddhism exposed all my fears, it also shed light on the parts of me that cared, wanted to survive, and still hoped to embody and experience love. Sitting with my feelings led me toward embodied loving, interdependence, opening, healing, and becoming. When I allowed myself the fullness of my feelings, I was no longer afraid of them, and I was able to see the impermanence of my fears.

This book will explore the many stages of feeling that I experienced after surviving the abusive relationship. We will visit the grandeur of a desert, the blossom of a flower, and the dual natures of an estuary. It is loosely based on the ten stages of loss described in the Westberg model of grief and loss,* though I wish to challenge any numerical and linear timelines of emotion and, by extension, life. I do not believe in feelings (or anything) traveling in straight lines. Instead, I see spirals, circles, eruptions, spikes, and waves of emotion. I believe that feeling is a perpetual moving cycle, where we meet ourselves repeatedly with compassion and

---

*The Westberg grief model is a modified version of the five stages of grief found in the Kübler-Ross grief model. You can read more about Granger E. Westberg's ten stages of grief in his book *Good Grief: A Companion for Every Loss.*

new insight. You can return to these chapters anytime, kind of like a Choose Your Own Adventure, except we never really get to choose.

Be Not Afraid of Love is an intimate swirling memoir of love, interdependence, and compassion. In recounting my personal story, it was difficult not to drown in shame or call myself stupid and deserving of harm. This is one of the lessons of the book, in understanding accountability without self-punishment or flagellation, and in devoting the same kind of compassion I had granted my abuser to myself.

This book is a meeting place. It is where we will explore the relationships between love and fear and where we will meet their many children. We will encounter all types of relationships: our relationships with one another, Earth, the systems that govern us, and ourselves. We are always in relationship, and we are always meeting again.

This is a story about rediscovering closeness in many forms, understanding our deepest fears, and believing wholeheartedly that we deserve the fullness of love. Be not afraid of what these reflections might reveal to you about yourself. No matter what you are afraid of, be not afraid of love.

Introduction

The Birth of
Love and Fear

I begin by telling you my story of survival, a tale that is unfortunately entwined with the first time I ever fell in love. My experience is one of intimate abuse, of falling in love and watching everything I thought I knew about love rot before my eyes. I wish to preface the tale with **trigger warnings**, to let you know that this story involves physical, sexual, and emotional violence and abuse. I will be using the letter "X" to refer to my ex-partner, who was also my abuser. I refer to him as X because I no longer wish to refer to him as "my" anything. The following incident happened during the second year of our on-again, off-again relationship. I have omitted some of the more graphic occurrences because I, too, am still in my spiral of processing, and there are some things my spirit is just not ready to share.

My story has multiple beginnings and endings, but I will begin on a dark night in Oakland, California.

Oakland is small, and everybody I knew usually attended the same parties and gatherings. That night we were going to First Fridays, the biggest monthly block party. The roads were closed, bars were open for happy hour, and local vendors were showcasing their small businesses down several blocks. Music was blaring from every direction and the smell of fried food wafted through the air. There was a festive atmosphere of celebration, and I was happy to be surrounded by familiar faces. I was with a group of friends, and we were drinking, laughing, and dancing from the moment we arrived. Soon after we made our entrance, I ran into X. We had been on break for a few months, and this was our first time seeing each other in a while.

Upon our reunion, our flame was quickly set ablaze. We were joyous, aroused, and anxious, and we quickly reconnected. My friends and I decided to continue our night at a bar, and I invited him and his friends to join us. Much to the disapproval of my friends, we started dancing together. They peered over my shoulder, eyeing him with caution and making sure that he was treating me with respect. They protected me more than I protected myself. After a while, the tension eased, and we were flirting and touching as if we had never been apart. We had the kind of relationship that was intoxicating and irresistible, and we had shared a comfort that felt easy to return to. We fed fuel to the flickering of our twin flame, and whenever one of us was ready to let the flame die, the other would reignite it.

My relationship with X was a dizzying cycle of perpetual intensity and yearning. We fed insatiable parts of each other's spirits because we had forgotten how to nourish our own. We thought we could not live without each other, but after a while that kind of living does not feel like living at all. We romanticized our addiction and misnamed it "passion," and in doing so manifested a toxic codependent relationship. Our addiction was fueled by our fears of scarcity, heartbreak, and neglect. We were addicted to the turbulent cycle, and we were fixated on looking at each other to avoid looking at ourselves. We kept dancing and I felt hot, indulgent, and guilty all at once. Whenever we were together, it felt as if I were in a trance.

Suddenly, he scurried away from our dancing. He was very drunk as he zigzagged out of the bar. His head drooped, and he was visibly shaking. It looked like he was having a drunken panic attack. When I called out his name, he sped up and slipped on the booze-drenched floor. I ran after him and could hear him furiously muttering under his breath, his face reddening with anger and embarrassment. I followed him out, my feet sticky on the ground as if the bar's gravity were pulling me back.

He was shaking with rage by the time I caught up with him. We were in the middle of the street. He looked over his shoulder to see if anybody was around. When he saw that the coast was clear, he dragged me aggressively by the arm into a dark alleyway. His grip on my forearm was tight and unforgiving, and I could tell that my skin was already starting to bruise from this sudden and brute force. I kept pleading for him to let go, but he would not. The alleyway felt like a vacuum; it was out of sight and sound, and dark as the night. I had been robbed of my senses. I could not see, hear, or understand a thing. Suddenly, sound returned to me, and his convulsed murmurs became screamed accusations.

"I know that you fucked a lotta people when we were apart!"

"Were you with a chink?!"

"I bet you slept with a bunch of girls, you fucking dyke!"

"Was his dick bigger than mine?!"

"You're a disgusting whore!"

His nonsensical slurs accused me of sleeping with a great number of people when we were apart. He had been so triggered by my presence that his paranoia was spilling out of him. The possibility of my forming relationships outside of ours felt unbearable to him, even if we were no longer together. In his mind, I belonged to him alone, and anything I did out of his control reflected betrayal. I could not speak, and I did not give him any answers. I was scared and confused, but I knew that I owed him nothing.

My silence alarmed him, so he grabbed my face and sank his fingernails into my cheeks. That is when I felt the first deep cut. He dug deeper and clawed at my face, scraping the dirt under his nails into my cheeks. He then forced my mouth open by shoving in his fist, searching for answers. He scratched the walls of my mouth and stretched my jaw wide until my skin and gums were torn and bleeding. I thought he was going to split my jaw in two, so I bit down, hard, leaving five pink crescent moons on his knuckles. First, taste returned to me, and my tongue could distinguish the mixture of his blood and salty skin. Then my sense of smell returned, and I inhaled the scent of whiskey on his breath. I started to feel my body again, and I felt burning and swelling all over my skin. My face was welting and stinging, and I began to unfreeze. I rummaged quickly through my bag and found my phone. It was dead.

I tried to get away, but his grasp on me was tight. I did not know where my friends were, and I did not know where to go. He called a car and said that we were going back to his house, no arguments. I silently obliged while devising a plan in my head. I slunk into the back seat, knowing that this was a risk that could endanger me in irreparable ways. He started making jokes with the driver, his voice clear and eerily sober. Hearing him laugh made me feel as if I were being choked. I could not muster the courage to cry for help. My voice was yet to return.

When we arrived at his house, he dragged me into his bed. I remember thinking, *This is the moment where I break in his hands.* I was acutely aware of all the sharp objects in the house, all the edges and corners, and all the different ways that I could either protect myself or die. I became alert to my bruised body, and how it felt naked, stiff, and small. He turned on his bedside lamp and saw the state of my face. I was bleeding. He began to weep.

He collapsed at my feet, bawling at the damage he had done. On his knees, he cried with despair and sobbed into my lap. I stared into space, absentmindedly stroking his hair. I felt nothing, and almost succumbed to an urge to comfort him, as if he were the one who was bleeding. Then I spotted a phone charger out of the corner of my eye. He was no longer gripping my body and had melted into a puddle of anguish on the floor. I swiped the charger and ran into the bathroom. I plugged my phone in and trembled while waiting for its light to flicker to life.

From the cold bathroom, I called a friend who lived nearby and whispered, "I've been assaulted. Can you help me?"

My friend was alarmed and called me a car immediately. I waited for it in the cold bathroom and finally saw myself in the mirror. My face was puffy and swollen, and my wounds were open and raw. There were cuts all over my cheeks, and the inside of my mouth was burning. I spat blood into the sink and gently wiped the gore from my face. Startled and in shock, I stared directly into my own eyes, searching for any spark of strength I could find. I could still hear his muffled crying through the walls.

Minutes later, the car arrived. I sprinted out of his family's beautiful old house. I ran past his childhood and graduation

photos, tokens of his adolescence, and remnants of our shared intimacy. I could smell old wood mixed with the scent of dried apples
and chilies, and I could still taste blood in my mouth. I hid my face
from the driver, and he worriedly asked me if I was going to puke.
I shook my head and fidgeted until we got to my friend's house.
The door was already open when I arrived, and I was immediately
enveloped in an embrace.

I wish that night had been the last time I saw X, but unfortunately, it was not.

For about a year and a half after the assault, I continued to see him
on-again, off-again, in secret. He called me a few months after the
attack, weeping apologetically and begging me to let him explain
himself, blaming it on the alcohol and his childhood traumas. He
love-bombed me and sent me excessive words of affirmation. He told
me I was special, that I was the only one in the world whom he had
ever loved and would ever love. I wanted so badly to believe him,
and so eventually I went back, sacrificing myself in the process.

During that torturous time, I stopped believing in most things.
It felt as if my spirit were torn to shreds, and I repeatedly ignored
my intuition. I was steeped so deep in shame, and ironically, the
only thing that could ease my shame was the insecure and fragmented promise of being "loved" by him.

He continued to mistreat me and violate me in predictable patterns, and I could always foresee my inevitable return to his arms.

I dedicated myself to taking care of him and made it my sole purpose to be compassionate toward his rage. I felt responsible for
him and detached from my own spirit. I felt hollow on the inside
and convinced myself that at least I was loved, at least I was loved,
at least I was loved.

Except I was not. Not even by me.

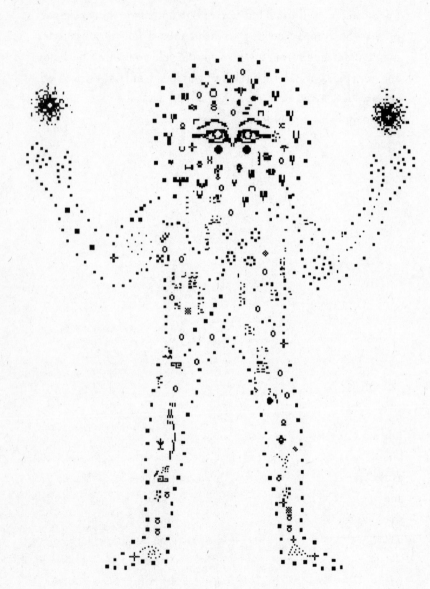

ONE

NUMBNESS

The Expansiveness of Feeling

Picture the sacred vastness of the desert. Driving past pink and purple dunes, witnessing the rock formations that tower over us as ancestors. I see the roundness of Earth, the globe that holds us, and the air that travels in billowing swirls into the beyond. The desert is typically described as the middle of nowhere, that there is "nothing" to do there . . . and yet all I can see is an abundance of space. I see expansion, shadows, cracks, time, and eternity stretching before me, and it makes way for all the things I cannot imagine but know lie ahead.

A year after the assault in Oakland, I went on a road trip with a friend to Arizona. We were at the Petrified Forest National Park, and we had gone on separate strolls, agreeing to reunite at a meeting place by a fence. We were surrounded by pink and purple canyons that were and continue to be shaped by the ongoing infinite nature of time. I knew how easy it would be to get lost, because the desert stretched into what a human could only register as an eternity. I was stunned by the desert's magnitude as I stood still in the silence of the sacred dry land. Surprisingly, I was not afraid of the abounding openness.

In what seemed like a bounty of "nothingness," I was overcome by a mélange of emotions. Every feeling I had been avoiding for the past year bubbled up in this "empty" space, somehow giving me full and unabashed permission to feel. It seemed as if I were being watched over, and the subtle hiss of the cracking earth was telling me something very simple and very true: *Open the space within you, because once you feel everything, you will let it all go.*

Following the assault, I experienced a year of staggered numbness. I thought that something was wrong with me because I felt so dead inside. I only experienced occasional outbursts of emotion that I would desperately try to suppress. My intuition was on high alert and always bracing itself for what was to come. The numbness was very unsettling, especially during the early stages of grief. After the assault, a dimness seemed to overpower the shock, and I was living in a perpetual pale and discolored period of emotional "nothingness." I was simultaneously disturbed by my subdued emotions and terrified to feel anything more.

There is a reason why numbness comes to visit us after we are hurt. Perhaps numbness does not signify a "lack" of feeling, just as deserts do not lack for life. Numbness is a compelling stage of wisdom on its own, and it offers an expansiveness that prepares us for the abundance of our feelings. Numbness does not have to be a blockage, especially if we honor its impermanence by not attempting to shorten or prolong it. There are millions of emotional possibilities that live within its spaces, and they are waiting for us to be ready to receive them. Numbness is an initiation that invites all our emotions to travel at their own sacred time. Just like the blessed desert, numbness is a force that invites us to acknowledge the eternity that stretches before us.

I thought that my numbness was an incapacity for feeling, a carelessness, and a reflection of a shallow form of love. I learned from the desert that my numbness did not illuminate how much or how little I cared, nor how deeply or shallowly I loved. It was not the extent of my grief, but it offered me a tender and spacious beginning. Numbness prompted me to tend to the life in my desert and prepare myself for feeling. The rain was quickly approaching.

Immediately after the assault, I could not conjure the words to name the violence that I had survived. The inside of my mouth burned with ulcers that X had dug open with his fingers. There were bruises on my body from being tugged, grabbed, and pushed around, ones that I would discover slowly in time. It was too painful to see my nude reflection in the light. I showered in the shadows, undressed in the darkness, and guarded myself from the nameless feelings that I wasn't ready to face.

Upon escaping X's house, I arrived at my friend's home and was rushed into bed. Four of my friends scrambled to hold me and started tending to my facial wounds, providing me with antiseptic, adhesive bandages, and pillows. They asked me what had happened and told me that it was okay to cry. I knew this to be true, but the tears would not fall. I was in shock, and robotically recounted the story, slowly recalling the dark alleyway, his sharp nails, and the sound of his sobbing. They listened in horror and shook their heads in rage and disgust. They consoled me, expressed their fury, held me until I fell asleep, and showed me a kindness and nurturance I could not verbally ask for. Each friend tenderly held my hands and feet and caressed me until I fell into a deep slumber. I dreamed of nothing that night.

The day after, we went dancing. Going to a party was my idea, and I pursued it with great urgency. I could tell that my friends were concerned, and they encouraged me to rest and asked if I was sure I wanted to be around a large crowd. I nodded desperately and searched for parties we could attend. I slapped a ton of concealer over my facial wounds and used adhesive bandages to hide the deep cuts on my face. The blood had barely dried. I wanted to be around as many people as possible to forget about my own fragile personhood. I said, "Don't let what happened to me stop us from having fun! I don't want to ruin our weekend."

I felt like a bruised burden, and in my refusal to become a victim, I neglected the tenderness of being a survivor. I wished to be surrounded by warm bodies so I could forget the freezing emptiness that rattled my own. I wanted to move my body because stillness was my sworn enemy. Stillness felt like an opportunity for my demons to swarm. I wanted to laugh to believe in the hollow timbre of my voice, and more than anything, I needed to stop myself from thinking about him. I shrunk myself because I thought that my pain did not deserve any expansiveness. I had no idea that my pain deserved to take up space too.

I do not remember much from the party, except for the countless comments I got about the Band-Aids on my face. We were at a bar that had a huge outdoor patio, and folks were approaching me in good spirits and calling the Band-Aids a "cute accessory." Whenever anybody asked questions, I would divert their attention elsewhere, or I would lie and quip about a friend's pet who had scratched me while we were playing together. I lied to people around me because I could not face a hard truth.

A vivid memory: a club remix of "Foolish" by Ashanti began blaring through the speakers. The song's buoyant beat could not hide Ashanti's lyrical yearnings. She was singing about a tumultuous and harmful relationship that she could not leave. Her words sent me into a panic, and I became dizzy and nauseated. A swelling self-destructive impulse bubbled up toward my throat. I recognized this itch; it was an anxious desire to call X and cry into his arms. I wanted to gasp for an explanation and plead for him to tend to the wounds that he had caused. I had to leave the party.

One of my friends followed me outside and asked me if I was all right, and I told her that I needed space. She sat me down on the cold concrete sidewalk, and after a few deep breaths, I began to calm down. I had snuck a drink out of the bar and downed it. My nausea and dizziness faded, along with my panic. Again, I felt nothing, and though it was brittle and jarring, I wanted it to stay that way.

For moments it felt blissful, as if I could play God and conjure a buffer between my feelings and my body. I reveled in these blank moments and thought about how I could prolong this temporary bliss. Subconsciously, I knew that my shock was wearing off, and my emotions were emerging in unpredictable jagged spikes, prompted by sounds, sensations, temperatures, and memories. I wanted to be numb forever.

After that day, I tried to drag the numbness out. I partied obsessively, pursued the fleeting highs of "retail therapy," and pushed myself into working on multiple projects at once, even though I could not focus on any of them. I pursued intimate relationships with anybody who showed me desire, to prove to myself that I was still lovable in my "brokenness." I committed to returning to "normalcy," and so I engaged in a performance of "reclaiming" myself.

I posted an image of my facial wounds on Instagram with a detailed account of what had happened. Because people could see it all over my face, I felt that I could neither escape nor ignore talking about it. I wanted to seem in control and did not wish to accept anybody's pity, so I hid behind a performance of being a "strong" survivor. It was important to me to show people that I was unfazed by the hurt and that X had no power over me. I did not allow my emotions to emerge because I did not want them to alter the rhythms of my daily life. I prioritized the presentation of "normalcy" over the raw realities of my emotions. By shielding myself from my feelings, I thought that I was protecting myself. My feelings were not my enemy, and they were not what I needed protection from.

My prolonged numbness was accompanied by its very own on-again, off-again lover: denial. I wielded denial as the weapon that would force my suffering to wave its white flag in surrender, ensuring my smooth survival. Many people had it so much worse than me, I thought. I told myself that the terms "domestic violence" and "assault" were too strong: it was a mishap, a lover's quarrel, a drunken mistake. The excuses became an armor that pushed away the pain, but painful feelings do not relent even when faced with brute force. They linger in the ether and visit you, whether you are ready or not to confront them. Denial masquerades as an accomplice to the expansiveness of numbness, but in fact it endeavors to break us into shards of our truth. By drawing enemy lines, denial is a refusal of our entireties. Denial is fragmentation; denial is desperate prayer.

There is a difference between honoring numbness and forcing it to stay. When I tried to prolong these periods of numbness by employing destructive and addictive behaviors, it became a means to avoid the complicated feelings that live within the shadows. Like the negative space of numbness, shadows do not signify lack, for there is an abundance that lives in the shade. When I make enemies out of my emotions, I push them further into forbidden unknowns, neglecting the crucial wisdoms that reveal my wholeness. Numbness is part of that, and this "non-feeling" is a vital time that needs to run its natural course. Numbness is preparing me for the dance of shadow and light. It is the opening of a vastness that will require much attention and tenderness. Sit with the numbness while it lasts, but do not try to control it.

My experience with emotional numbness felt like a double-edged sword. On one hand, the initial effects of numbness protected me after the assault because the wound was so raw. On the other hand, I became dependent on the comfort and began to manipulate numbness to my will. I wanted to be numb whenever I was conscious, and I was terrified of the emotions that unexpectedly emerged. After a long and enduring period of numbness, I sank into depression. I began to ask myself why I could not feel anything, what was wrong with me, and whether I would feel anything (especially love) ever again. Everything felt simultaneously arduous and dull. I had pushed my emotions so far away that I thought I had lost all ability to feel. I rode the motionless wave. At the time, that was all I knew how to do.

My numbness was like the expansive desert, and in its shadowy stretches, the earth was cracking beneath my feet. My foundations of love, companionship, and self-assurance were fractured, and my emotions were waiting to emerge. What life was arising from the cracks in my foundation? I had to find non-extractive tools and support systems to help me face my fears. Survival is not always a showcase of resilience, but a trembling, expansive, unstable journey that requires vulnerability as strength. I had to be brave enough to face my emotions. In the Petrified Forest, I was summoned to a halt. I had to listen carefully to the wisdom coming from within.

When I returned from the Petrified Forest, I knew that I had to ask for help. I needed guidance, both through the emotional dry spells and through the impending avalanches of feelings. I learned that seeking help to soothe myself was nothing to be ashamed of, though I knew that I needed to adopt some alternative methods. The coping mechanisms I had used were the same ones that mainstream Western media taught me. Clearly, they were not working. With as much courage as I could summon, I started to seek talk therapy and looked for a counselor who specialized in clients who experienced intimate partner violence. After much trial and error, I finally found a therapist who is queer and Asian, and who works with an organization that offers free counseling to people who need it.* She encouraged me to journal my stream of consciousness and practice being nonjudgmental toward myself. It helped me profoundly.

We need to seek alternative ways of bearing our emotions. We deserve to feel the fullness of our feelings without self-destruction, scrutiny, and shame. We need to destigmatize the idea that we experience our hardships in isolation. We need to build supportive mental health networks that understand how dark and intrusive our feelings can be, while also being aware of how exhausting and destructive it is to run away from them. We need mental health care that is accessible and affordable, and we must move beyond escapism and consumerism as our core coping methods. Practicing nonjudgment and compassion toward ourselves and one another will allow us to sit with our numbness and be prepared for our emotions as they arise. Going deeper, we can ask ourselves: What tools and resources do we have once the numbness begins to fade? Why have we been taught that being "productive" is the way to tend to our open wounds? How do we care for ourselves, and one another, when the feelings come to light?

There are many plant medicines that induce numbness in the body. Cloves, for example, have antibacterial properties that can

---

*I am very grateful to the New York City Anti-Violence Project.

be used to treat oral and gum pain. When crushed and mixed with the enzymes in your saliva, they tend to create a numbing effect that eases discomfort in your mouth. Szechuan peppercorns produce intense levels of spice and heat that are followed by tingling vibrational sensations on your tongue. The soothing properties of aloe vera create tranquilizing relief for burns and injuries of the skin, the largest organ of your body. Numbness induced by our plant relatives reassures me that numbness is a natural sensation of the earth that can aid us in our healing.

It is a blessing to experience relief from pain. A tingling, a soothing, or a vibration generously gives us a chance to momentarily divert our attention from physical pain. Herbal medicine allows our cuts and wounds to remain while they aid in the regeneration of our physical vessels. Our bodies, too, can create natural numbing sensations when our blood circulation is cut off or when our nerves are pinched, creating a chrysalis of temporary pins and needles. Numbness is not a sensation merely created by man-made machines. It is a lesson found in the natural world when personhood meets pain.

What about our emotional pain? Do our emotional responses follow the wisdoms of our plant siblings and bodies to conjure numbness in the face of bereavement? Do our brains try to comfort us just as much as the outstretched arms of an aloe vera plant? Just like our plant kin, our emotional reactions generate a tingling wave of numbness. However, the numbness usually wears off, opening the space for us to notice and tend to our heartache and allow the feelings to surface. The temporary numbness that both the earth and our bodies grant us shows us that numbness is an ancient, familiar feeling, and that much lies ahead of these passing moments of calm. How, then, can we express gratitude for these temporary stages of numbness without becoming addicted to manipulating them?

Emotional numbness has now been manufactured and reproduced on a global scale. After the assault, I tried very hard to get a prescription for any kind of benzodiazepine. I wanted to be as sedated as possible. I could not obtain a prescription because I did not have American health insurance. Because I had no money, I was deemed unworthy of treatment, which reaffirmed that pharmaceutical companies offer medicine only to those who can afford it, just so that they can sell more.

The book *Bad Pharma* exposes the capitalist pharmaceutical industrial complex in the United States. According to its author, Ben Goldacre, a former doctor, "Some have estimated that the pharmaceutical industry overall spends about twice as much on marketing and promotion as it does on research and development." It seems to me that many manufactured numbing agents are inseparable from the agenda to accumulate wealth and capital.

Consumerist numbing tools such as television and social media are designed to be pacifiers of emotional pain. They were not invented out of care for people's wellness, and instead are used as active and purposeful agents to inflate the economy. Because Western society has labeled emotions as weak or "unproductive," it is within the capitalist's agenda to void them all. To these companies, heavy emotions interfere with work and jeopardize the machine that many of us are unwillingly a part of. When we prolong our numbness, we must interrogate the forces that encourage us not to feel. By promising us a swift return to states of "normalcy," capitalism takes advantage of our natural desire to soothe our wounds. Capitalism seeks to replicate numbness not to heal, but to ensure that we can continue working and consuming to avoid pain, which is deemed unproductive.

Manufactured numbness looks like a blue screen. Our phones have become prominent numbing agents of our everyday lives, feeding into our addictions to consumption. We open an app on our phone to read the news and then flip to a different app to block out the traumatic information. In 2018, I attended a class called #divestfrominstagram that was hosted by Neema Githere with their grassroots collective Radical Love Consciousness. Neema radicalized how I thought about and experienced the internet and opened up a crucial communal conversation.* They taught me how to name my toxic relationship with social media, and critically analyze the ways that the algorithms are designed to tap into my addictive desire for escape.

Social media and I have a toxic relationship, as I alternate between absorbing violent news and consuming entertainment and humor within a matter of minutes. Now more common and accessible than any form of medicine, social media has become the perfect sedative. By overwhelming us with a dizzying fuzz of content, the worlds inside our phones are in constant movement. When we look away, we are unable to sit still.

Social media encourages us to avoid the messy, unpalatable, and unpostable portions of our existence by making everything presentable. We become addicted to living vicariously through people who perform their versions of joy and success. Even marketed portrayals of survival ask us to idolize the "glamorous"

---

*To support more of Neema's work, go to their Linktree: linktr.ee/finding neema.

survivor who created a business and continued working despite experiencing violence. The glamorization of the "girl boss" has encouraged survivors to exploit our own trauma to build empires. Social media can never fully communicate the nuances of what it means to be a survivor because it flattens our messy and painful experiences into two-dimensional pleasing performances. While social media is a valuable tool for finding community and resources, it is merely a starting point and not a means to an end. It is only one dimension of many, and we must learn to establish firm boundaries within these virtual worlds that encourage us to consume our own suffering.

The capitalist state does not want us to look deeper. Consumerist healing offers unnatural solutions to our pain, while refusing to admit that these systems have caused so much of it. People who have been deeply traumatized by colonization, war, and violence have been in post-traumatic shock for generations, while capitalism expertly endeavors to pacify intergenerational pain and create more cycles of addiction. Furthermore, corporations attempt to sedate hurt people who deserve healing, and get richer from profiting off the pain that they have caused.

The process of finding adequate and nonexploitative physical and mental health care in America is difficult, and natural alternatives are often inaccessible and not a part of public education. It is worthwhile to question capitalism's relationship with numbness and the intention behind inventing numbing agents that are marketed and sold worldwide. How does it feed into our relationship with numbness? How can we find alternative ways to heal physical and emotional pain—not only the pain caused by personal trauma but also the pain inherited from intergenerational systemic harm?

Despite all of this, most of us still need to seek help from state-sanctioned health care because it hoards medicinal resources and technology. There is no shame in having a prescription for medication that is helping you get through each day. However, we must constantly interrogate and critique these systems and their intentions. The system fails us again and again and creates the illusion that we are the ones who are failing.

Grassroots community organizing has shown me that there are alternatives: nonaddictive and communal methods to healing that do not rely on the state. There are many mutual aid networks all over the world that guide people through trauma and grief.* For example, I have seen queer Black, Indigenous, immigrant, and non-Black people of color healers redistribute natural medicinal plant care packages to marginalized and traumatized folks.† I have seen Traditional Chinese Medicine practitioners offer free acupuncture, cupping, and healing. In *Care Work*, disabled nonbinary writer and disability justice movement worker Leah Lakshmi Piepzna-Samarasinha describes mutual aid as "voluntary reciprocal exchange of resources and services for mutual benefit. Mutual aid, as opposed to charity, does not connote moral superiority of the giver over the receiver." Mutual aid healing networks provide peer-oriented systems for support when the numbness subsides. Mutual aid is antithetical to the pharmaceutical industrial complex

---

*In later chapters and at the end of this book, there is information that leads readers to online mutual aid compilations by the incredible organizers of BUFU (By Us For Us) and their extensive community, holistic healing resources compiled by Studio Ānanda, as well as mental health resources for survivors compiled by Natalia Mantini of Solace.

†The Herbal Mutual Aid Network (HMAN) is an incredible grassroots organization that provides free plant-based medicine for Black people seeking support due to racial violence and abuse. Learn more at hman.love/.

because it intends to abolish hierarchy and profit to create new possibilities of healing together.

Numbness is a time of preparation for abundance. While it is important to recognize our numbness as a crucial stage of healing, it is also important to remember that we do not have to do it alone. Numbness is found within the sap of the earth and the blood that runs through our veins. It is protective in spirit and guides us toward the continued work of true healing. We must learn to discern between natural and manufactured numbness, and honor natural numbness as a call for tenderness with one another and ourselves.

As I stared into the abundant desert of the Petrified Forest, my wave of numbness wore off. I did not run, and I did not reactively check my phone. I looked at the dry crackling earth beneath my feet and the expansiveness it offered me in the stillness.

In *The Smell of Rain on Dust*, Martín Prechtel describes the importance of numbness in grief. "It is a time of natural molting," he says, "where the armor of rational thought is pulled away long enough to give us the necessary space of time, in which we are open and unhardened enough to let our new vulnerable state and its soft new skin surrender to grief's able handling of the rudder of our little ship of sorrow and loss."

I am learning from each crack in the earth that numbness is an opening, an emergence, and an awakening. It is natural to be numb, and it can be harmful to prolong emotional numbness in the name of avoidance. I must be wary of the addiction to the fuzzy manufactured nothingness because the numbness is not supposed to last forever. Our relationship to numbness is a reciprocal one that roots to our survival. It allows us the space to lovingly prepare for something profound.

In my numbness, I saw the desert within me and what I needed for the long road ahead. My numbness created a home for my difficult emotions to blossom into love and self-forgiveness. My numbness was preparing me for the downpour of rain.

As I stared into the abundant abyss, my body remembered, and my spirit prepared for release. It just needed to make some space before the rain began to pour. My pain was expanding, and it was filling me up. I felt myself expanding too. I was remembering myself.

I began to sob and choke and cry. I was ready for my feeling.

TWO

ANGER

Giving Life to Vital Breath

T he Chinese characters for anger, 生气 (shēng qì), relay a poignant translation of the nature of rage. Each Chinese character represents its own being, element, or sensation, and when combined, they create new and poetic verbs, feelings, and meanings: 生 (shēng) means to "give life to," and 气 (qì) means "a vital breath," or "air," which is the same 气 (qì) that you find in the beginning of 气功 (qì gōng), the popular traditional Chinese movement meditation that works with redirecting bodily energy and breath. When conjoined in a dance of new meaning, not only do these two Chinese characters 生气 (shēng qì) mean anger, but they also literally translate to the poetic phrase "to give life to a vital breath." This definition has helped me see that anger holds a sacred life of its own. We are responsible for bringing anger to life, and life to anger. Rage is a sacred and necessary energy that is part of our being, and part of Earth.

Anger is often seen as the villain. It sprouts from seedlings of fear and is frequently born of an urgency to protect and dignify what you love. It works with many different emotions and manifests expressions such as resistance, action, revenge, violence, and protection. Anger lives in pulsing relationship with other complicated feelings, such as sorrow, shame, and insecurity. Because it can be such an overwhelming and powerful feeling, it is helpful to pay attention to what other emotions it is working with; otherwise, anger can become impulsive and dominating. When we think of anger as a vital breath, we must think about the source of its power and what we express in each sacred exhale.

Can we consider anger a loving force? You are rageful, you are fearful, you are protective, and you are also loving. All of these truths coexist. At the core of a love-based anger, we are fighting for our sacred survival. Love encourages us not only to protect ourselves but also to honor our being and all that we are in relationship with. When we cannot acknowledge the love that holds our vital breath, we are overtaken by a fear-based rage that drives us toward feelings of resentment, shame, and vengeance. During a discussion for the podcast *For the Wild*, Lama Rod Owens said, "Anger is the bodyguard of our woundedness."* Anger, like numbness, is another sacred protector of our survival. It is a loving act to

---

*You can listen to and read the transcript of the podcast episode titled "Lama Rod Owens on Liberatory Rage/191" at *For the Wild*'s website: forthewild .world/listen/lama-rod-owens-on-liberatory-rage-191.

protect yourself, a loving act to resist harm, and a loving act to allow yourself the sacred breath of anger. Everything brings us back to love.

There is no emotion I would ever tell you not to feel. I do not write to encourage you to overcome any emotion. Instead, I encourage you to sit with each emotion. Perhaps even go deeper. There are so many short-term and buyable solutions to anger, anxiety, and depression that encourage us not to feel, or to "transcend," negative thought. This ostracizes us from our own feelings and from people who are experiencing heavy emotions. When somebody feels deeply hurt or betrayed, it can be a harmful response to tell that person to immediately "overcome" or "be above" their painful feelings. Each feeling we hold is the natural conjuring of an energy that exists within us, though that feeling is not all of us. Emotion is energy, and energy is a vital part of our life force.

I like to imagine every emotion as a vital sacred protector, an ancestor embodied as a feeling, telling me in their own language what I have been taught to overlook. They all have homes within us. Anger is the sacred breath that we must allow ourselves to release, for it holds a vital truth about what truly matters most to us. Anger is an invitation to connect deeper with yourself and to uncover what you are trying to protect. Are you trying to protect something that your ego is attempting to control, or are you trying to protect your sacred beingness and all that you love? What are you willing to let go of, and what are you willing to fight for? Anger is the powerful force that allows us to bring violent systems of harm to their destruction, while also giving breath to loving possibilities of creation. Allow yourself to breathe.

The first time X and I spoke about the assault was three months after it happened. I was thousands of miles away from Oakland, in my childhood home in Australia, because I needed to be close to familial support. Each morning at the crack of dawn, I woke up from fuzzy and indecipherable nightmares, which I would later learn was a symptom of post-traumatic stress disorder (PTSD), covered in sweat, my heart trembling with palpitations. Each night X came to visit me in my dreams, and even though I could not see him or speak to him, I could sense that his lingering presence was there.

One night, I dreamed of heaven. This rococo-style paradise was adorned with blushing opal skies and sunbeams that flirtatiously peaked through flocculent fogs. I was standing on one particularly illuminated fluffy cloud, blissful and wondrous, gazing at an eternity of dramatic pastels. As I peered into the dreamy abyss, I saw a figure in the distance. It was X. For the first time in months, I could see his face. He was not alone. He was encircled by crowds of people; I recognized some of them as mutual friends whom I had talked to about the assault. They were applauding him, adoring him, and celebrating him. Then they all turned toward me and scowled. It became clear that this was his sanctuary, and I was an intruder.

I woke up in shock, feeling betrayed and confused, and drenched in cold sweat. I was terrified of the vivid sight of his face, both strange and familiar at the same time. For some reason, he still felt close by. I checked my phone to bring me back to reality and, to my dismay, his name was there. Two missed calls and a text message. He had called while I was dreaming of his heaven. The text message simply read "I love you."

My shock bubbled into a palpable rage, and my anger took me by surprise. All the anger I had suppressed came seething to the surface. I wanted to yell at him and demand justice and repair. I wanted to hear him grovel and beg for my love. I decided to call him.

"HOW COULD YOU DO THIS TO ME?!"

"IF YOU LOVED ME, YOU WOULDN'T HAVE HURT ME!"

"WHY DID YOU WAIT THIS LONG TO SAY SOMETHING?!"

I had nearly forgotten that X was on the other end of the phone as I screamed, distraught and choking on furious tears. For months I had sat ashamedly in a thick stew of my emotions, not allowing rage to come to the surface. I had told myself that I was above anger, that becoming rageful was only "stooping to his level." I thought that getting angry would make me as violent as him. All these sentiments were birthed from the murky depths of shame, a place where I redirected all my rage toward myself.

He stammered a helpless "It wasn't me . . . that's not who I am . . . I don't know what came over me." He blamed his violence on the alcohol, and I could hear that he was in denial about what he had done. During the assault, it seemed to me that he had been possessed by an otherworldly force. This is what happened when he did not endeavor to understand his anger; it became a stranger even to him. I spent what felt like a lifetime trying to solve the riddle of his rage because he was too afraid to know it for himself.

"IF IT WASN'T YOU THEN WHO THE FUCK WAS IT? YOU ARE A GOOD-FOR-NOTHING ABUSER WHO DESERVES TO ROT IN HELL."

I was light-headed and under a spell of my own. All my furious thoughts were escaping their cages. I felt dizzy, delighted, powerful. Through the avalanche of feeling I allowed myself a moment of monstrosity: I realized that I *did* want to hurt him in return. There was a tip in the scales, and now he seemed almost afraid of me. I relished the feeling. In the shape of these outrageous words, the anger expelled itself from me, like poison. I started to sob.

For a long time after this call, I thought that I was a terrible person for all the livid thoughts and feelings that flooded through me when I spoke to X, but then I realized that these reactions were only a small part of my expansive vitality. I've since learned that when rage overtakes me, I must remember that I am not rage in full totality. I am a being who *experiences* rage; rage is a vital part of my emotional expansiveness that is deserving of healthy release. I have to express my rage in safe and sacred ways. When I honor my rage, the anger simmers into a clarifying energy, one that works to act for change.

Truthfully, I deeply wanted things between us to change, and I wished desperately for our love to be reborn. It took me a long time to understand that my safety is my number-one priority. The will to change my circumstances needed to start from the protection of my well-being with safe distance and firm boundaries. X's rage had nothing to do with me and was also not my responsibility to heal, especially because my safety was at risk. His rage had developed a life of its own inside him because he had no healthy ways of releasing it. Either he forced himself to not feel his rage or he forced it upon others—and that is abuse.

While honoring anger is important, it is not an excuse to be harmful. Safe ways to honor our anger include expressing that anger in solitude, in journals, in unison with others, with support by our side, through dancing, singing, or yelling into the void. To honor anger in our loving relationships, we must let it simmer before we communicate our frustrations. We must breathe our vitality before we scream it.

During the assault, I was forced to witness X's explosive rage, which he misdirected toward me. When his rage erupted into violence, it had long fled from love and was heavily entangled in fear. Because he had not processed his anger from traumatizing childhood experiences and betrayals, the attack was a moment when all of it was released at once onto me. Rage is sacred and should be honored when expressed; honoring the rage means understanding it as an emotion, not a call to be violent or hurtful. When we do not take the time to honor our rage, fear and hatred can become its driving forces. A violent expression of rage that is not self-defense stems from a hateful desire to replicate harm.

One of the first responses to being hurt is the desire to reproduce the wound. By re-creating the pain and inflicting it on somebody else, a person close to you, or even yourself, you enter a cycle of punishment. Cloning pain can create continuous cycles of violence. Each person has different ways of processing hurt, and all the heartaches in our lives form delicate relationships with one another, creating a chain of painful entanglements. The longer the pain is avoided, the deeper the resentment becomes. This sequence can last for generations and often does when not attended to.

My rage often makes me uncomfortable, especially in the face of conflict. When I was growing up, I witnessed a lot of misdirected rage in my household. I saw how my immigrant parents would quietly bear being humiliated in public and then return home to replicate that harm with each other. I was so terrified of that anger as a child that I hid from it. Instead of expressing my anger directly, I learned to convey it in passive-aggressive ways. There is a common misunderstanding that passive-aggression rises above feelings of anger, but it really is an avoidant strategy to suppress it. Because I had never felt safe expressing anger when I was growing up, I became very fearful of any escalation of conflict and misled myself into believing that anger was futile. What I did not know was that if I wanted my anger to pass, I had to let it be felt in the first place.

Passive-aggression does not endeavor to protect the spirit; if anything, it attempts to prove itself "above," or avoidant of, rage. Passive-aggression tries to protect the image that I wish to maintain of myself. It is dishonest not only with the people who have hurt me but also with the self. It tricks me into believing that it is superior to the perceived erratic frequencies of rage and asks me to numb and mute the validity of my anger. When we convince ourselves that we are "good" people who are beyond "negative" emotion, we suppress vital parts of ourselves that are deserving of communication and expression. It can be an act of love to confront somebody when we feel betrayed by them if we are transparent and centered in our intention to express ourselves, and not focused on punishing the other person or replicating harm. When we believe that a good or perfect world is one that has rid itself of anger or sadness or death, we become fearful of the radical teachings within these natural experiences and emotions.

While it is important to honor anger as a sacred protector, it is vital to distinguish harmful, manipulative, and violent expressions of anger (especially those turned into abuse) from self-defense and protection, particularly in relationships. We need spaces that encourage nonviolent expressions of anger so that we do not go home and misdirect them violently at each other. Just because anger is sacred and comes from a deep place, it does not make abusive expressions of rage okay.

Perhaps X was protecting his inner child from abandonment triggers and believed that all his past wounds had compounded his rage. Whatever the case, it was not okay, and it did not come from love. One of the most manipulative things an abuser can say is that they hurt you because they loved you. It is quite the opposite; they hurt you because they hate themselves. When we fear ourselves, our actions and outbursts become unrecognizable, even to us. X did not have enough compassion to care for or process his own hurt. He had never been taught how. It is not the survivor's responsibility to figure that out, even though we often think that it is. Nobody should be the scapegoat of anybody's self-hatred.

Who is permitted to feel safe in anger? Who can safely and publicly express the sacredness and power of their rage, even when it is nonviolent? It feels irresponsible to tell anybody to be angry without acknowledging that there are certain privileges in being able to openly express difficult emotions. Survivors navigating abusive relationships often do not feel safe expressing their rage in order to protect themselves. When, and if, we do, we could be put in even more danger, including being condemned by the state.* No matter how infuriated, hurt, and terrified I was, I never felt safe expressing my rage to X.

When I was growing up in Australia, my Chinese parents told me to move through rage in silence, to never publicly announce it, and to reserve it for when I got home. They told me that it was a way to protect myself, especially in the face of racist white Australians. They said that it was best to never give racist white people a reason to retaliate. They passed on their protective wisdoms, which were part of their survival too. As a result, my anger hid in the shadows, and I silently carried it within me, even while I was being harassed. The unexpressed rage became my own burden to bear, and as a result I misdirected it toward myself. Violence often happens behind closed doors because the suppressed anger misdirects itself toward the people we should be holding close.

White (which includes white-passing) people, regardless of whether the motive behind their rage is violent, misdirected, or well-intentioned, have typically been able to express their rage publicly because of the privilege that protects them from state-sanctioned punishment. White anarchists will quickly and furiously burn corporate establishments to the ground, igniting fires and

---

*You can read more about the criminalization of survivors of domestic abuse in #SurvivedAndPunished: Survivor Defense as Abolitionist Praxis, which is a collaborative tool kit created by Love & Protect and Survived & Punished. Read it here: survivedandpunished.org/wp-content/uploads/2018/06/survivedandpunished_toolkitbw.pdf.

starting protests without intentional safety guidelines, and in doing so endanger the marginalized people around them who are being targeted by the police. Racist white murderers are often so twisted by their misdirected rage that they can freely publish violent manifestos without being held accountable for them. Black people, especially dark-skinned Black people, are not afforded the same privileges in being able to safely express their anger. Racist and colorist anti-Black carceral systems in America target and demonize Black people as "aggressive" and "violent" for expressing any emotion at all.

Anger cannot be typecast or flattened into a single dimension of being. In his book *Love and Rage*, Lama Rod Owens writes about the ways that people, especially Black Americans dealing with racial injustice and trauma, can navigate rage as a wise and generative emotion, not only to demand justice but also to express ongoing and ancestral grief.

> We must allow the anger to be in our experience. I continued on and spoke about letting ourselves be angry as the first step to healing the hurt that is beneath the anger. I talked about my anger and how learning from my anger about all the hurt inside me that the anger was covering. And that if we don't wrestle with anger, we never get to the heartbreak. And if we don't get to the heartbreak, we don't get to the healing.

Instead of demonizing or typecasting the rage of the survivor, it is transformative to listen to the anger that demands urgent accountability and change. I am grateful for Lama Rod Owens because he speaks of anger as an emotion that uncovers vulnerability, joy, and a will to heal. Anger is a voice that speaks for the pain of grief and the softness of compassion. Demonizing and shaming anger as aggressive and irrational takes away a person's agency to feel those feelings, and further corners them into isolation. When somebody is nonviolently expressing their anger, it can be transformative to hear their concerns and get to the depths of their heartache by providing them with emotional support. We need safe spaces where survivors can feel supported and not judged or vilified for their rage. Anger can be a force of revolutionary love, and branches out from its core into many other dimensions. When anger is used as an action toward liberation, the intent is not just to destroy but to nourish the fertile soil that is left in its wake, blossoming into new loving ways of thinking, feeling, and being.

Contrary to popular belief, hatred and anger are not always comrades. Anger can be dismissed as the antithesis of love, and I have often found it problematic when self-help books talk about anger as if it were a disease. We cannot ascend beyond anger, nor avoid it, and it is very useful to understand it and not conflate it with hatred. The mixture of anger and hatred is what creates violence, not anger and love. In her essay "The Uses of Anger," Black feminist poet Audre Lorde writes, "This hatred and our anger are very different. Hatred is the fury of those who do not share our goals, and its object is death and destruction. Anger is a grief of distortions between peers, and its object is change."

When anger propels radical nonviolent change, it is a force fueled by love. I keep returning to the Lama Rod Owens quote "Anger is the bodyguard of our woundedness" because I feel softened when I read it. I think of turtles with their hardened shells protecting their squishy bodies. I think of deer antlers and rhinoceroses' horns, and how protection is a part of survival. I think of the thorns that prick up from the stem of the rose or the body of a cactus. If we live, there will be forces we need to protect ourselves from. If we live, we will also find ways to express and liberate ourselves. Our rage is a sacred protector, and we must live with it as such, as just another part of our sacred, soft, powerful, and squishy spirits.

Misdirected and unprocessed rage is the cause of so much violence. Sometimes, when we are fearful of understanding our anger, we do not tend to or process our wounds, and unconsciously we begin to replicate those wounds in the people closest to us. When we avoid our woundedness, the energy of rage is transformed into a spiteful lust for violent vengeance.

Martín Prechtel wrote in *The Smell of Rain on Dust* that "once a show of destructive power and death-dealing becomes an accepted attempt at a 'solution,' a victory that can be celebrated without the grief of funerals is never possible, because whosoever is forced to kill or destroy another's life is forever entangled with the spook of what they have destroyed." I think this is an extremely poignant telling of what karma really is.

Lama Rod Owens speaks of karma in a profound way, drawing on what he has learned from his Buddhist practice.* According to him, the Western world's definitions of karma do not adequately

---

*Owens talks about this on the podcast *For the Wild*, in the episode "Lama Rod Owens on Liberatory Rage."

describe the complexities of karmic energy exchange. Karma is not the retaliation of nature, nor is it as simple as when one person does a bad thing and then experiences a bad thing as punishment. It is spiritually deeper than that. Karma is the idea that somebody must live with the pain and grief of harming someone, as harming others is ultimately a form of self-harm too. By having to live with the harm that they have caused, and not seeking guidance or accountability to atone for their wrongdoings, they fragment their own spirit because they damaged somebody else's. This sets in motion a dizzying spiral of violence because harm is inherited in so many ways. Abusing others inevitably means abusing one's self.

After the assault, I became obsessed with wanting to hurt X in return. I had to ask myself during these harmful impulses if I would truly feel better, safer, and fulfilled if I did. Would my spirit be healed, and would I feel whole? Would his suffering tend to my wounds? I knew that if I endeavored to punish him to seek some kind of vengeance, I would still be neglecting my own wounds. Creating more harm would only obstruct me from the tender healing that my hurt required. Instead, I had to look deep within. When the anger emerged, I had to express it nonviolently by journaling, ranting, thrashing, and singing poorly at the top of my lungs. I refused to express my rage toward him in a violent way because I knew that by doing so I would also hurt myself.

Abusers hurt themselves when they hurt others. Violence is reflected within the fragmented soul of the person who perpetrates it. What one does to others, one inadvertently internalizes and does to oneself. X's rage might have developed from heartache, but his violent reaction turned his rage into destructive hatred. He expressed a rage that did not will for change, and because he refused to understand his festering wounds from childhood and previous relationships, he became obsessed with replicating them. I represented the closest semblance of love and hate in his eyes, so much so that it confused and triggered him, and so he chose to replicate his wounds within me. He tore himself apart in the process, further deepening the wounds in himself.

Abusers are often survivors themselves, and while they require help in ending their cycles of violence, the person who is enduring their abuse cannot be the one to tend to their wounds. One of the reasons I felt so attached to X was that I had assigned myself the role of his helper. I could see the way that his violence twisted him up inside, and I wanted to be the one to save him. All the while, I was being hurt and dragged through emotional, physical, and sexual abuse, and used as a scapegoat for his internal self-hatred and raw woundedness. I had to learn how to prioritize *my* self-protection and survival. He needed help and so did I. While my compassion allowed me to understand X's pain, I had to practice directing compassion toward myself. I needed to dedicate my nurturing energy toward myself, which meant that I could no longer be the helper and that I needed to ask for help.

To honor rage, we must allow it to see the light. Like a deep exhale, anger can escape the fortresses of our bodies and come out of the shadows. Anger is a reaction to betrayal, sadness, and yearning, and our bodies remember it and store it deep within us. Anger needs to be expressed healthily without violence and with care.

Instead of trying to suppress or avoid anger, we can try to see it with softness. Where is the rage coming from? What wounds is anger trying to protect? And how should we release this energy from our body safely and responsibly?

We must commit to building a world where we can all experience the freedom of nonviolent expressive rage in safety. We need to build a place that does not define justice as seeking revenge, punishing, and replicating harm. We can learn from the masters of qì gōng (气功) who move and release the stored sacred energy that lives within us. While we breathe life into the vitality of anger, we must also allow that breath to flow into all our being, and to go deeper into the wounds that need tender tending to.

Now when I am angry, I get to know my rage as more than just a reaction. I scream into vast and open spaces, I process it out loud, I thrash in rapturous dance, and I scribble furious thoughts into the sacred seclusion of my journal. As I practice healthy expressions of anger, the anger flows through my entire body. It triggers old betrayals and new sensations, and I must allow the impulse for pettiness or retaliation to pass. Anger has given me permission to have a full bodily cry, and it has given me the drive to fight for my survival. It draws boundaries, makes space, and illuminates difficult truths. Not only does anger allow me to give life to vital breath, but it also allows me to see how sacred my breath is in the first place. Anger is not an irrational fear but a luminescent passage that brings us back to love. Anger pushed me to leave X and finally return to myself.

As I write this, I am angry, and from each rageful word flows a deep inner compassion, the softness of my wounds, and the demand for radical and urgent change.

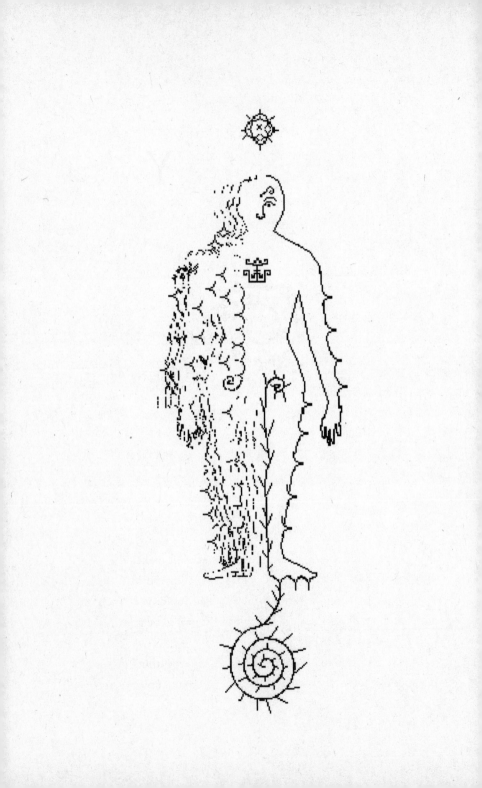

THREE

ANXIETY

An Unknowing of My Own

nxiety feels like time travel. It takes us out of the present and propels us into a buzzing, turbulent, time-hopping mode of existence. When I am anxious, I throw myself into perpetual fantasized futures and alternate timelines. I run in reverse toward the heaviness of my past, determined that history will repeat itself. It makes me forget about each glorious breath because it catapults me into horrific imaginings of when my breath will cease. Anxiety expects the worst and hopes for the best, but it never seems to be able to focus on the now.

Anxiety instills an urgent need to control everything around us because it fears so deeply the instability of the unknown. It forgets that there are some things we simply cannot predict or manage, especially when it comes to other people's actions. When we discern what we can and cannot control, perhaps our anxiety will ease, we can let go, and our focus will sharpen. Anxiety challenges our relationship with control.

As a survivor, I know that the harm I survived was undeserved and uncontrollable. Sometimes, however, I felt as if I had lost control over my coping mechanisms and reactions. My anxiety was so severe that it drove me into the static of chaos, and I was terrified of diving into the unknown, trusting my instincts, and relearning a new reality. I had to start small, like learning to control my breathing and turn my shallow breaths into deep ones. Heading into the unknown is a trust exercise, and I had to slowly peel myself away from toxic attachments to reclaim my agency. Though I could not unbreak my heart, I slowly learned how to soothe it.

Anxiety is prickly and resides all over the body. Amid the time travel of anxiety and the chaos of panic, the most helpful thing I can do is ground in the moment. While everything shifts so scarily in unexpected ways, I must remember that the most consistent present truth is that I am here. You are here. Each worry is valid and uncontrollable, but what soothes the spiky feeling is having faith in its passing. The spiral of anxiety does not begin with my anxious thought but with the being who is experiencing it. The spiral does not begin with despair but with the person who embodies and eventually overcomes it. I am not my anxieties but the awareness that is experiencing them. I cannot control my anxieties, though I can be aligned with my awareness. I am as enduring as the ocean and my anxiety mimics its movements: coming, going, and washing away.

7:45 a.m.

Every morning for six months after the assault, I woke up at 7:45 a.m. in a sharp panic, feeling as if I were suffocating and gripping my palpitating heart. If it was because of a bad dream, I could hardly ever remember the nightmare upon rising into consciousness. The anxiety did not come from the dreamscape, but from the panic of returning to my waking reality. A fear pulsated through my days, and it was at its most intense in the morning and late at night. Panic engulfed my spirit, though I could not figure out exactly what I was so afraid of. I was back home in Australia, and we were an entire ocean apart. X could not physically be close to me, and yet it always felt as if he were right by my side. Each morning my heart would pulsate and pitter-patter, and all my senses were inundated with a heightened awareness of their functions. I was swallowed by an aliveness that made me want to die.

I revisited journal entries that recollected the anxious questions that I agonized over every day.

> What if he's with somebody else? What if he's hurting them? Why doesn't he love me? Why couldn't he love me? Do all our friends still love him? Is everybody hanging out with him? Why do I still love him?

I was afraid of my fear and its unfamiliarity. I had never experienced a post-traumatic fear so intense and entangled with residual loving feeling. It felt uncontrollable and foreign, and in my most vulnerable state, I craved the exact opposite: to be in control and with the familiar. Even though it was torturous, his abuse had become my norm. During early morning anxiety attacks, my body was experiencing symptoms of withdrawal from the violent familiar. Separating from X meant that I had to relearn love and intimacy, and my anxiety came from not believing that I could (or deserved to) experience love again. I felt as if I had to start anew, and the thought of that terrified me.

My shadows were so unexplored that I continuously looked outward and fixated on him as an external element that I could potentially control. I wanted to know every detail of his life because I did not want to leave any space for my unknowing. While I was trying my best to distance myself from him, I was faced with the frightening reality that I did not know life without him as both my lover *and* my abuser. I was panicked because I was horrified of X and his misdirected rage, and I was also anxious about our separation, coping with the abrupt and necessary end of our relationship. This duality spawned a space of unknowing that seemed too contradictory to confront.

Each morning's panic attack felt as severe and confusing as the next. Even though I had blocked X, I still checked my phone each time I woke at 7:45 a.m. to see if he had tried to contact me. Nothing. I would always be relieved and disappointed at the same time. His abuse had become so normalized that I did not know how to function without it. I was scared of finding out who I was without him. I secretly hoped that he would find a way to contact me, as he had done in the past. Did his lack of contact mean that he no longer cared? It took me a long time to digest the idea that his control and lack of boundaries were not a form of care.

Because he had been so controlling during our relationship and so paranoid about my every move, I realized that I been robbed of my agency for a very long time. My choices had been devoted to his being, his pain, and his healing, and suddenly having to make my own choices was alarming. There would be days when I'd be intensely anxious about him showing up and violating me, and there were days when I would miss him and worry about him being with someone else. The dichotomy of my love and fear was entranced in a chaotic feverish dance, and in the brief moments when I was not afraid of him, I was terrified and ashamed of myself.

I was traveling through life on a timeline that was not my own. I was fixated on his future because I did not want to process my past. I was convinced that I would never be in a healthy loving relationship because I was "damaged" and emotionally unavailable. The possibilities in his life felt more vivid and imaginable than my own future. Even when I was a continent away, I felt neither liberated nor free; instead, I felt so out of control of my own being because he was no longer in control of me. I was at a loss. What followed our immediate separation did not feel like freedom, but instead felt like an extended shadow of confusion, numbness, fear, and anxiety that made me terrified of letting go. Releasing the relationship would mean relinquishing my control over the familiarity of our life together and beginning to know and live my own.

Intimate violence and abuse are a specific type of harm because the violence is inflicted by somebody you love who you thought, or wished, loved you. They have violated not only you but also the sacredness of the relationship. The foundation of relationships is meant to be safe: a celebration of the sanctity of each other's being, and a commitment to protecting each other from the violent forces of the world. You share experiences that illuminate the purity of presence, and memories that hold magic. A safe and stable foundation does not mean perfection, nor is it free of mistakes, misunderstanding, and hurt, but there needs to be a baseline and a mutual understanding that you will not violate each other, even when your feelings start to change. Abuse within intimate relationships ruptures all sense of safety and distorts the promise of trust. It consequentially makes the safe relationships of your future seem like unfathomable fantasies.

I wish to be clear about my definition of intimate partner violence, based on my own personal experiences: within my intimate and romantic partnership with X, I experienced multiple levels of violence, including emotional, physical, and sexual abuse. It is important to note that intimate partner abuse can show up in many ways for people in toxic relationships. I do not believe that all harm can be lumped together. For example, the repercussions of emotional abuse differ from those of physical or sexual abuse. And the reactions that survivors have to the varied levels of harm experienced—such as anxiety, PTSD, self-harm, and addictive coping mechanisms that are connected to past trauma—are different. Even though these levels of harm are nuanced and personal and cannot be lumped together, I do believe that all of them are survived by people who did not deserve any of it, and therefore are worthy of healing and care.

The conversations surrounding surviving abuse are usually steeped in stark binaries. Either the survivor leaves or the survivor stays. Either the survivor is safe or the survivor is unsafe. The implication is that once the survivor leaves, they are safe, and it is assumed that once the survivor leaves, they are free.

It is more complicated than that. Just because a survivor has physically left an abuser does not mean that they feel safe in public, in new relationships, or even in their own bodies. Physically leaving an abusive relationship is certainly the miraculous beginning of healing and could potentially save a person's life. However, it may take a long time after leaving for the survivor to genuinely feel safe and free in their body. The emotional distancing and detachments that are required can take years to achieve. Long after my relationship with X ended, I lived with anxiety, PTSD, and a strong distrust of future relationships, especially with men. Even after I physically left him, it took me years to feel emotionally and spiritually safe in my body. It took me a long time to truly let go.

A lot of mainstream media talks about abuse by centering on the abuser and the assault, without exploring the very long and intense emotional, spiritual, and psychological aftermath for the survivor. Many long-form documentaries about intimate partner violence almost seem to sensationalize the abusers, and they can be very difficult for a survivor to watch. Survivors are depicted either as helpless and pitiful victims of their own poor choices or as resilient troupers who make capitalist empires out of their pain. These narratives seem to be fearful of shedding light on the nuanced aftermath of abuse because it is neither marketable nor "tragic" enough. I am dissatisfied with the ways that survivors have been disregarded and even ridiculed in the media, and not seen as full, complicated, and traumatized people in need of healing. I am tired of survivors being seen as worthy of love only when they have the courage to leave and condemned when they are held hostage.

There are some incredible works that focus on survivors' nuanced narratives and experiences, such as Michaela Coel's British TV series *I May Destroy You* and Carmen Maria Machado's book *In the Dream House*. Both shed light on how complex it is to unlearn the familiar patterns of abuse and how self-realization is not a series of consumptive habits or wins. Instead, healing from abuse is a rough and anxious journey of relearning love within yourself. Both Coel and Machado explore the complex emotions that arose from the vast unknowing that they were faced with when everything they knew about love was destroyed.

When I made the conscious choice to block X, I felt a little safer but a lot more anxious. Having contact with him at least allowed me to know where he was and what I should avoid. After the assault, I always wanted to know X's whereabouts so that I could calculate my own moves. It did not seem fair to me that he was probably somewhere enjoying his life, while I was suffering from heartbreak and PTSD. Not knowing his whereabouts meant that there was so little that I could control. Not knowing meant that finally, after a long and painful relationship, I had to devote my attention to my own spiritual and physical safety, which was something I had forgotten how to do.

Returning to myself felt like an insurmountable challenge; my agency and spirit were unrecognizable to me. I wanted to understand a violence that felt implausible. While I obsessively tried to rationalize the reasons X hurt me and the origins of his pain, I realized that I was still too scared to look at my own hurt. I had stigmatized myself as a broken victim of violence and therefore as someone unknowing and unworthy of love. My unknowing was my enemy, and as I endeavored to destroy it, I became obsessed with controlling everything around me so I could be as vigilant as possible. Knowing became my weapon because it granted me control. Obsessively theorizing and managing everything only made me even more anxious.

My anxiety quickly manifested as mania. I refused to be still because I was perpetually terrified of the unknowing that would catch up to me. The anxiety felt like a blot of ink on delicate parchment, spreading itself like a foreboding shadow. It heightened my instincts to run, and so I darted toward a fabled finish line that would promise me any form of certainty. I did not allow myself to wander in my unknowing because I was frightened that the worst was hidden in the shadows. I wore my body down by constantly partying, taking substances, working tirelessly, and throwing myself into shallow relationships based on physical desire. At the start of each morning and at the end of each day, my swirling thoughts arose from the darkness, and I would plan my day to align with a determined sprint for distraction. I was exhausted. I am not shaming myself for my coping mechanisms. I am naming them because it has taken me so long to become aware of them. This naming is honoring the unknowing that I had at the time, and how I was so unaware of the ways that I was surviving. Not knowing then allowed me to know what I do now.

Nobody is afforded the luxury of consistent knowing. Our knowing shifts in every moment that we are present, which is why we so often latch on to what is familiar. During an abusive relationship, a survivor's knowing can be completely distorted, where abuse becomes the most consistent thing in our lives. The repercussions of the abuse are gradual, and all that we know slowly shifts while our sense of self-worth deteriorates. While we become familiar with knowing the conditions of abuse, we can no longer recognize ourselves. To come out of these toxic cycles, we must prepare ourselves for the periods of unknowing that are awaiting us. We must support one another in these times of unknowing by not enabling destructive behavior and listening to these moments of emotional eclipse. While there is so much that we cannot possibly know, we must be certain of one thing: we are worthy of love, and abuse is not love.

In *All about Love*, bell hooks* defined love as a verb and wrote, "[Love is] 'the will to extend one's self for the purpose of nurturing one's own or another's spiritual growth. . . . Love is as love does. Love is an act of will—namely, both an intention and an action.'"† I often contemplate this definition and learned that spiritual growth needs to be reciprocal within any loving relationship,

---

*Sadly, bell hooks passed away as I was finishing this book. She profoundly changed so many people's lives, and she completely radicalized the ways that I move through the world with love. Naturally, her incredible work is weaved throughout this book, and I would not be the writer I am without her generosity and tenderness. May she rest in peace.

†She quotes M. Scott Peck's *The Road Less Traveled* in this definition.

whether romantic, platonic, or familial. While I became aware of the lack of reciprocity and respect in my relationship with X, I still found myself missing him. I had to ask myself: If it was not a whole and healthy love, then why was I craving his love so much? Why was I so afraid of not knowing life without him? And if what we shared was not true love, then what was I still so attached to?

Detachment does not happen overnight and requires a lot of time and patience. To detach myself from X, it was helpful to analyze and learn about our attachment styles. Whenever we spent time apart during our relationship, he was intensely anxious and suspicious about what I was doing without him. I was both anxious and avoidant, uncomfortable with his attachment to me and too anxious to vocalize my needs or separate from him. Because we were both enraptured in this toxic anxiety-inducing dance, it was difficult for either of us to end our relationship. After a while, we were all we knew.

In the book *Attached*, psychiatrist and neuroscientist Amir Levine and psychologist Rachel S. F. Heller break down the three major attachment styles established by Mary Ainsworth and John Bowlby, who studied the Western psychological science of adult attachment: **secure attachment**, **anxious attachment**, and **avoidant attachment**. Additionally, another attachment style was later discovered by Mary Main and Judith Solomon—the **fearful-avoidant** style, which vassilated between anxious and avoidant tendencies. Your attachment styles are subject to change throughout your life, and they operate on more of a spectrum than as strict categorizations.

If you feel secure in a relationship—interdependent, emotionally available, and ready to provide for a partner's needs without neglecting your own—then you have a **secure attachment**. When you deeply crave partnership and intimacy but are also insecure and terrified of abandonment, overcompensating in relationships and blaming yourself for any conflict that arises, you have an **anxious attachment** style. This attachment style can manifest as paranoid, self-deprecating, and controlling behavior. On the other hand, if you have an **avoidant attachment** style, you may act as if you were emotionally unavailable, withholding, and afraid that a committed relationship will compromise your individualist self-sufficiency. You often still seek relationships because you secretly crave closeness but suppress your desire for intimacy out of fear and insecurity.

I found learning about attachment styles helpful because I recognized my own behaviors in all of them. While these attachment styles can serve as general guidelines, they are not definitive. Being able to read about how I adapt to relationships allowed me to see my mutability in the face of fear and love. Attachment styles extend outward to family, friendships, and even our relationship with the state. By observing these behaviors, we can see the parts of ourselves that are reacting from places of fear, childhood trauma, and anxious insecurity.

People with **anxious attachment** styles have often faced abandonment in their lifetimes. Familiar with neglect and heartache, they have been conditioned to think that they exist to please others. Taught to believe that they are only lovable when loved by others, they find it hard to consider that they are worthy of pouring love into themselves. They have a difficult time handling the frequencies of unknowing and can sometimes lash out when they think that their security is compromised. Often they place their safety into the hands of their loved ones and act out in ways that appear needy or demanding. When they feel their partner pulling away, they can become controlling, obsessive, and manipulative. People with anxious attachment styles are usually reacting out of a deep-seated fear that comes from a place of scarcity when they hurt others.

People with **avoidant attachment** styles are not that different. They fear closeness not because they resent intimacy but because they, too, are afraid of abandonment and heartache. They do not want to be left, so they leave first. Or they stay emotionally detached and unavailable to avoid getting hurt. This nevertheless reveals a deep yearning to experience closeness, and an incapacity to accept that they are deserving of it. They can also act out in hurtful ways by disengaging during communication or leaving abruptly. People with avoidant attachment styles usually do not allow themselves to deeply connect because they think that it makes them weak and codependent. They subscribe to the notion of hyper-individualism and do not believe in the possibilities of interdependence. They also have a hard time believing that they deserve to be wholly loved.

While I was learning about attachment theory, I found that I resonated with emotional tendencies exhibited by both the anxious and the avoidant-attached. Upon reading *Polysecure* by Jessica Fern, I discovered the fearful-avoidant attachment style, which was not mentioned in *Attached*. According to Fern, people with this attachment style "have the characteristics of both the dismissive and preoccupied styles—their desire for closeness and their longing for connection are active, but because they have previous experiences of the ones they loved or depended on hurting them, they tend to feel uncomfortable relying on others or are even paralyzed by the fear that speaking their feelings and needs could be dangerous and make things worse." This helped me understand a lot of my own behaviors within so many of my relationships. I often vacillated between fighting for someone's affection and withdrawing when it was time to receive it, as if I did not believe that I deserved it. The healing of this attachment style required me to learn how to receive affection from myself.

X and I were in a relationship that triggered both of our attachment styles. I always thought that I was saying and doing something wrong and began to believe that I was a bad partner and deserving of harm. I avoided communicating my deepest needs and desires because I feared his reactions. I spent so much time tending to his emotional needs that I assigned myself the role of his caretaker. I almost derived a pleasure from it. I constantly tried to impress him, and I found it difficult to sever our ties because the anxious part of me was attached to my role as caregiver and the consistency of our relationship. I was anxious about my staying, and he was anxious about my leaving. If he did not know my whereabouts, he would text me and call me a hundred times. We both saw this happen with our immigrant parents, and so we replicated it with each other. It seemed normal, and we even foolishly called it "passion." We both wanted answers to the questions that remained open from our childhoods without realizing that we could only seek those answers by wholly loving ourselves. We latched on to each other because we were both conditioned to think that was love.

Because X was so afraid to lose me, he did everything he could to control me. When I was with him, I felt materialized, fetishized, and itemized. I felt like X's favorite toy, dismantled and dragged on the floor, and always there to hold at night. There were many factors in his life that were unstable, and his means to control me was a way to escape the tremors of his uncertainty. I was the embodiment of stability in his life, so I was treated as an object that could never leave his side.

We were stuck in a loop of chasing our anxious and desperate dreams of "love." I was anxiously attached not only to him but also to the constancy of his daily abuse. Even though abuse is often unpredictable, I noticed that there were consistent rhythms within his patterns of harm. He would be anxious and not communicate, then he would resent me, and then he would lash out. After that, he would apologize profusely and love-bomb me, becoming overtly attentive and caring. The cycle would repeat itself until it became familiar. It mirrored cycles I had witnessed growing up, and so I stayed attached, because I did not know much else.

All endings and transitions create thick fogs of uncertainty. Each time our relationship ended, there was a rupture in the pattern that created a time of unfamiliarity. Leaving an abusive relationship is the first step on an unknown arduous journey of healing. Detaching yourself from the relationship is the hard part that comes next. Cutting our emotional and spiritual cords was the initiation of my true emotional, spiritual, and physical freedom. I needed to see that the shadow is survivable, and that I did not have to go through it alone.

Secure attachments require reciprocation and support. These relationships require both parties to be affirmed in their own worth and excited by the promise of sharing life with each other. Instead of trying to dominate or control each other's moves, securely attached partners move with a mutual ebb and flow. In *Attached*, Amir Levine wrote that "secure people feel comfortable with intimacy and are usually warm and loving." As a person who has endured intimate trauma, I can say that it is not always easy to get there. When we are stepping into the eclipse of the unknown, we require strong support systems to relearn openness with intimacy. We need material resources, therapy, and honest guidance to unlearn toxic attachment styles. We also need to work on nurturing secure relationships with ourselves. Though it takes time to become securely attached, half the work is realizing that you deserve to feel secure in loving relationships.

In the foreword to *The Politics of Trauma*,* labor activist Ai-jen Poo writes, "There are things we have control of in life and things we don't. . . . We cannot control the actions or behavior of others— but we do have agency over how we respond to those actions." As a survivor, I cannot control the hurt that I have experienced, though I can control how I choose to heal and act in future relationships. While it felt as if I were losing so much of what I knew, my unknowing held the promise of my coming closer to health, care, and safety. Even if I knew nothing else, I was nearer to believing that I am worthy of love.

Worry is often a companion to frantic everyday life, especially alongside securing food in your stomach, a roof over your head, clean drinkable water, and necessities for survival. These essential

---

*The Politics of Trauma is a book that radically shaped the ways I've learned about healing, and I highly recommend it. My friend Niki Franco introduced the book to me via her Venus Roots book club and I am eternally grateful. Shout-out to Niki and check out her book club at patreon.com /venusroots.

resources are hoarded by systems that were built to protect prop-erty, not people. In contemporary late-stage capitalism, states have deemed small exclusive groups of people worthy of wealth, forcing those who are not born into generational affluence to participate in the dizzying contest of upholding the economy instead of one another. At the top of the hierarchy lingers a group of people des-perately clutching at their monetary stability. Considering the tight, white-knuckled grip these people have on their wealth, I could guess that they feel anxious too. It is now normal for every-body to feel anxious about the increasing unknowing of everyday reality. It can be hard to feel safe with each shallow breath.

Detaching myself from my toxic relationship with X allowed me to analyze the other harmful relationships in which I am deeply entrenched. For example, our relationships to the state, to coloni-zation, to capitalism, and to money are all relationships that feel harmful and impossible to walk away from. How can we navigate these abusive systems that deliberately try to unnerve us? How do we leave these complicated relationships when they are thor-oughly entangled in our everyday survival?

My relationship to money has always been strained and painful because I grew up in a household where money was scarce. This instilled a perpetual scarcity mindset within my immigrant family, and anytime small bursts of wealth came our way, we always felt as if we were going to immediately lose it all. Consumer culture cre-ates anxiety-inducing conditions that force people into survival modes rooted in scarcity. The system forces people to stay in per-petual and exhausting cycles of work. We have been taught that the only way we can gain stability and abundance is if we earn it, and to prioritize our relationship with money above all else. Be-cause we must now navigate so many structures that seem to be out of our control, finding little moments that we can "control," such as intense hoarding and addictive splurging, can feel temporarily rewarding. We may not necessarily love the things we buy or hoard, but we adore the sense of control it provides in uncontrollable conditions, although we may find that it never feels like enough.

Our craving for stability reflects the dissatisfaction of our current constructed realities. We want stability that is not determined by a supremacist state. Whether we are latching on to money, material items, or one another as anchors to this earth, our dread informs us of a need to find control amid undeterminable circumstances. We cannot put our lives in the hands of those who wish to dominate us, and our collective restlessness shows me that we wish to break free. Once we do release ourselves from the constraining reins of the state, we will have to navigate much uncertainty. How, then, will we deal with what feels like the utterly uncontrollable? In our scrambling search for stability, we must remember that the most powerful and beautiful process is the continuation of life. As we move with the swirling forces of radical change, the most constant grounding force we can return to is our breath.

Anxiety, like numbness and rage, allows us to allocate what we deeply care about. Amid our global crisis, it is almost impossible not to care. We are anxious because we are affected. Earth is crumbling because of anti-Indigenous violence and reiterations of colonization. We are watching our children grow up dependent on the consumptive dimensions of cyberspace, and we are seeing movements around the world fighting for justice that long ought to be just. A domino effect is produced because these abusive systems rely on one another to persist. We are experiencing collective PTSD, except the trauma seems to keep going, and adequate treatment is difficult to come by. There are some things we can control and some we cannot. For example, we cannot control the avalanching consequences of humankind's actions, but we can control our awareness and commit to doing better for sacred Earth.

In its own erratic ways, anxiety is another ball of energy that brings us closer to our care. If we discern within our anxiety the small things that we can control, then we can urgently act on those things. I refuse to believe that we are doomed because our collective anxiety shows that we care. I refuse to succumb to despair because our worry shows me that we no longer wish to be controlled. I believe that our connected awareness and collective action can take us there. While we observe our feelings without judgment, we can relinquish the idea that we know everything that the future holds. All that we can know is what we care about and how we lovingly choose to hold it close.

During my healing journey, I was enrolled in a free acupuncture program offered by the Anti-Violence Project. I was still experiencing ripples of PTSD symptoms such as anxiety, vivid flashbacks, and dissociation. The trauma still lived in my body. I desperately needed support and still found it extremely hard to ask my friends for guidance, so I turned toward this incredibly generous organization for help. I shared my experiences with my counselor, and she kindly enrolled me in free group acupuncture for two weeks.

Acupuncture is a practice in Traditional Chinese Medicine (TCM) that involves placing small needles in specific pressure points on one's body.* Acupuncture is helpful for people who are experiencing chronic bodily pain, PTSD, and anxiety. Western medicine has dismissed TCM as "nonsensical" or "savage" because it is an ancient and ancestral Chinese practice. Western medicine treats one's pain like an enemy, fighting "the enemy" until it (and its surrounding parts) die, whereas TCM treats one's entire body as a friend and soothes every interconnected part. TCM profoundly acknowledges that our heavenly bodies are constellations, and that treating one body part inadvertently benefits another. Our anatomy forms intricate constellations within us, from foot to liver, temple to teeth, neck to ear to heart.

My acupuncturist was a queer Korean person who always ensured that everyone in the group felt comfortable and safe. With their care, they made the process as easy and painless as possible. Before each session, they briefly taught us about our bodily interconnections by showing us a diagram of the constellations of our pressure points. They taught us that the ear is deeply connected to the brain, and so they chose to focus on our ears to connect to the parts of our brain that respond to trauma. The ear is an intricate maze of acupressure points that target both physical and emotional pain. They placed four delicate needles into different points of my ear, including a point in the upper fold called the "heavenly gate." Stimulating this specific point helped relieve the prickliness of my anxiety.

---

*When exploring TCM, try to support Chinese, Asian, Asian American, Black, and Indigenous practitioners. I have included some resources for TCM at the end of this book.

Every time the needles were placed, it felt as if my body were experiencing a huge rush of release. A wave of calm would always encompass my being, and I would feel a tingling sensation that ran from my ears to my toes. It is rare that we are given the opportunity to be this still with our own constellations, and the needles allowed me to be present with them while calming my tendency to overthink. My mind became genuinely quiet, and I often drifted peacefully into sleep. There were times I cried because the needles prompted a natural release, an opportunity for the frantic energy of my anxiety to dissolve into tears. In that room, I gave myself permission to feel what I needed to and care for what I love. I realized how much I cared for myself, and how there were people who barely knew me that cared for me too. Acupuncture gave me the opportunity to be still, even in my worry, and it taught me just how much sitting with myself could soothe me. It allowed me to connect the dots of my bodily interconnections and think about how sacred I am.

Going to group acupuncture taught me that seeking support is a fundamental part of survival. Everybody in the group came as often as we could, and though we did not know one another's experiences, none of us judged the others for being there. It was a safe space that allowed us all to heal without judgment, and to cry with the sacred medicine in our ears. Once or twice, I cried just knowing that there were people around me who were experiencing soothing reprieve from the pain in their lives. We were allowing our bodies to connect the dots within us. It was healing to see people engaging in mutual aid and opening themselves up to the unknowns of the healing process. There is a growing abundance of resources for survivors by survivors, and it is imperative to continue doing the work for one another and ourselves. It is beautiful to know that we can collectively find reprieve through the murky unknowing.

Acupuncture did not provide me with any answers to my burning questions about X or my future. The needles did not present me with theories or epiphanies or logical facts. Instead, they allowed me to experience blissful moments of stillness and gave me clarity on what I could and could not control. I could not control my circumstances, though I could consciously develop a constant practice of presence and gratitude. During my sessions, I was no longer time-hopping and found myself deeply present in the now. My addiction for the toxic familiar was momentarily soothed. This precious skill echoed outside my sessions too. Acupuncture nudged me to walk toward my unknowing with the assurance that I had a support system during the process. The delicate little needles gently prompted me to appreciate my life, body, spirit, and mind that were all brave enough to continue. It showed me the miracle of my existence at my very own heavenly gate.

FOUR

GRIEF

All Endings Must Be Mourned

F unerals have always frightened me as grim and formidable events. They remind us of injustice and mortality, and they reveal the inevitability of death. Death is simultaneously so simple and so complicated, and while we cannot romanticize grief as a mere celebration of life, it's a crucial time for our deepest expressions. Those of us who continue to live must take our time to send sacred spirits to their afterlife. For years, I treated grief as if it were an unimaginable taboo. I raced toward mythical sunny utopias where sadness does not exist. I tried to escape the grief that required me to facilitate many funerals in my head. I have spent so much time running away from my looming grief, sprinting toward a purely joyful existence with intrepid speed. When I looked back at the tiny speck of me, I saw with widened eyes my deep neglected grief and my flowing sadness: the only thing I distanced myself from was me.

The Western world is obsessed with binaries, splitting joy and sadness into enemies. Life and death are classified as direct opposites too. Human beings have long understood the ecstasies of happiness and the heaviness of sorrow. Joy never ceases to be beautiful, while grief never seems to get easier. Binaries create fragmentations and opposing forces, and do not regard joy, sadness, life, and death as intrinsic to the wholeness and balance of being. While sorrow and death are difficult and scary experiences, instead of being taught how to feel and navigate them, we fear them so much that we strive to completely avoid them. It is not surprising that in the Anthropocene, human beings are obsessed with inventing technologies to achieve immunity to both sadness and death.

Ocean Vuong wrote, "Too much joy, I swear, is lost in our desperation to keep it."* If we befriend only what feels good, we alienate our hurt. When we are judged by others and ourselves for weeping about separation, heartbreak, trauma, tragedies, accidents, and death, we push vital parts of ourselves away. The binaries of good and evil categorize our difficult feelings as evil and our happy feelings as good. When sorrow is seen with self-judgment, it can generate a great sense of fragmentation within. Suppressing our sadness can grow into a cruel cynicism, making us scared of our own feelings and doubtful of the fullness of life.

We are taught that grief is dysfunctional and unproductive and that it gets in the way of our work. Or we are encouraged to milk our grief and capitalize on our experiences, generating trauma

---

*From his debut novel, On Earth, We're Briefly Gorgeous.

porn for the masses to consume. Either way, we are dissociating from grief and isolating ourselves in the process. When I was presented with the urgency of my mourning, I did not know what to do with my feelings. Instead, I dedicated myself tirelessly to work, to production, to proving myself immune to suffering. Even though death is inevitable, and loss occurs every day, it seems that we are less equipped to deal with it than ever.

When our grief is neglected and unfamiliar, we begin to isolate ourselves in confusion. We cannot see that there are whole and multidimensional beings around us who have experienced heartache, and we become ignorant to the fact that we can be supportive to one another during these painful times. In a world dominated by performances that encourage us to portray ourselves as our most joyful, we begin to assume that everyone is free of grief. Perhaps we just want to cry with one another without judgment, or weep by ourselves and know that we can process our grief with somebody we trust. What happens when I am no longer embarrassed by my grief, and I am surrounded by humans, plants, and animals who hold me while I cry?

Amid our tumultuous global circumstances, we are experiencing much collective premature and unnecessary loss. Ironically, we are losing so much because of greed. We are in collective mourning, and we need to acknowledge our grief without exploiting it. Right now, collective grief is just as important as collective joy. Grief is an ancestor who teaches us to exercise constant and immense gratitude. Funerals are opportunities for us to express unconditional love. There is much to learn from swimming in the deep shades of our grief, and we will emerge from it basking in the sun. If we cannot honor our endings, then how are we supposed to usher in new beginnings?

I spent six months after the assault in my family's home. I wanted to be around my loved ones, though I barely ever spoke to them about my emotional and mental health. I spent most of my time in numbness and shame, pushing away my feelings and spiraling through sporadic episodes of fury, anxiety, and remorse. I missed my friends in the Bay Area and I was getting restless. I told myself that I did not want to be inhibited by grief, and that I had to hurriedly move on with my life. I felt stifled by my life at home, and so I made plans to move back to the Bay. I was determined to return stronger than ever—I would do whatever it took. I resented the idea that X's presence could stop me from going back to a place I loved and I wanted to prove to myself that I could mend my relationship to the place where X had tried to break me.

I felt fearful of returning, but I dismissed those worries as weakness. I was rushing myself, disallowing any crucial reflection that would show me that I was not ready. I wanted to prove something not just to myself but to my friends, my family, and, most of all, X. I wanted to act as if I were unscathed and renewed, ready for a brand-new chapter—when in fact I had not even processed the last. I told myself that I was refusing to allow X to carve out my fate. I resisted my own hurt and still subconsciously centered him in my decisions. I lived in active resistance to him, which still made him the central figure in my life. I had forgotten who I was without him.

I did not allow myself to feel sadness because I did not want to be a weak survivor. I was reacting from a place of hurt without ac-knowledging that I was in pain. I told myself that any tears I cried for him would be tears wasted on a man. I tried to satisfy my ego by performing a heroic version of myself that I wanted people to perceive. I wanted to prove to my friends, my family, and fellow survivors that I could make a speedy recovery and overcome the abuse with as little mess as possible. But grief is messy, and survival is complex, and I was not on my own healing journey; I was on a journey that was sold to me. I felt pressured to conform to a speedy and clean recovery that required no true vulnerability, grief, or ug-liness. I did not allow myself tears or solitude, and soon I began to control and dismiss myself in the very same ways that he did. Be-cause he was no longer around to police my feelings and actions, I sat in as a substitute and policed myself. I did not realize that the tears I needed to cry were not for him. They were for me.

What I was not telling anyone was that I missed him deeply. The assault put an abrupt end to our on-again, off-again relation-ship, and it was difficult for me to even consider mourning the re-lationship at all. I missed him and hated myself for it. The thought of missing him felt so violent that I actively pushed the grief away. The complicatedness of healing from an abusive relationship is a dance of love and fear. I wished that he had never been my abuser or my lover, but the complex truth is that he was both. I fantasized about forgetting him and once again pushed my mournful feelings to the side. Even though the end of our relationship was necessary, it was still an ending. All endings need to be mourned.

Though I did not permit myself to miss him, my yearnings were triggered by random everyday occurrences. It was as unex-pected as the whiff of a bakery, the sound of skateboard wheels on gravel, or the chorus of a song. It was the sight of a bicycle, the fuzzy scratch of a record, or the gentle autumn breeze. I bad-mouthed him to my friends in public and then went home and ashamedly swatted away fantasies of our tender loving moments. In those rare moments of solitude, it felt unbearable and shameful to miss him. For those reasons I refused to be alone. I would shake my feelings off by telling myself repeatedly that missing him would make me weak, an apologist and an enabler.

Repressing our emotions is a common survival tactic because sometimes these feelings are too painful to bare. Other times, it can be because we do not wish to face the judgment that we assume will be passed on to us, by others and by ourselves. I was judging myself much harder than anyone around me. I felt as if I had a dirty little secret.

A month after returning to Oakland and settling into a new home, I found out that somebody had told him that I was back. I panicked. X knew where I was, and he felt close by. Now I no longer had distance to protect me, and I was both tantalized and scared. My anxiety was so inflamed by that knowledge that I convinced myself of a way to take control of the situation. I sent him a text: "I know that you're aware that I moved back. Please keep your distance and leave me alone." To which he responded, "I love you. I want to see you and apologize."

All my suppressed yearnings were reignited. It was because I had quashed my tender feelings that they overwhelmed me so quickly and suddenly. My memories of us in love grew into a romantic montage, and I no longer wanted to resist my cravings. All that I had pushed away, all the sweet memories that I had disallowed myself to recollect, became even more idealized and forbidden. His text had triggered a part of me that I had buried long ago, the part of me that missed him in my loneliest hours. As all my unprocessed emotions dawned on me, I realized that I wanted to see him again. I forgot that he was my abuser and could now only remember him as my lover. As I sprinted from one polarizing extreme to the other, I found myself running right back into his arms.

Soon after, we met at a park. All my neglected emotions—sorrow, rage, longing, desire—rose to the surface, and when I saw him, they all snowballed into one. We spoke for a while and caught up as if nothing had happened, and then with as much sincerity as he could muster, he began to apologize for the assault. He told me that he had been intoxicated and had stopped drinking since, and that after the assault he had gone into hiding and not interacted with anybody for three months. My intuition warned me to keep my distance, while my yearning for familiarity inched closer toward him, absorbing every promise and apology that he made. I ignored my intuition and succumbed to my longing, and soon after hearing his apologies we kissed and slept together the same day.

I want to be clear that I do not wish to glorify or idealize grief. Grief is difficult and messy, and mourning an abusive relationship is never going to be a pretty or romantic process. All my yearnings came as a surprise to me because I refused to feel them in private. I did not allow myself space to feel them, and I rushed myself into a state of reclaimed "normalcy." It was an act of dishonesty to deny that X held deep significance to me. He was my first love, no matter how hard I tried to deny that. I truly loved him and therefore needed to mourn what we had shared. Instead, I buried those feelings with defiance, and when I saw him again, all those unprocessed emotions rose to the surface. Because I did not allow myself enough time to grieve him, my emotions were triggered and expressed in chaotic, unexpected ways. I did not know that missing somebody is necessary to the process of letting them go.

We embarked on a secret relationship that lasted for months. The rekindling of our fire was painful and destructive. While I thought that our reunion might heal my wounds with the myths of closure, my heart was perpetually broken. Continuing this relationship felt like scratching at the wounds from the assault and, sure enough, my spiritual and emotional wounds continued to bleed. Our toxic cycle was in full swing, and we prolonged the relationship at the risk of destroying both of us. We did not go anywhere in public and booked hotel rooms whenever we wanted to spend the night together. I would block him whenever I felt ashamed of my actions and then unblock him whenever I felt vulnerable, scared, and alone. It was dizzying, toxic, and turbulent, and we did not know how to stop.

The only light I saw was in the rare tiny slivers of joy that we'd experience together. We could only afford those brief moments when we both stepped into willful ignorance, and once that blissful second was up, one of us would be resentful, angry, and hostile again. Depression anchored me to the familiarity of our relationship and coerced me into feeling "secure" within our insecurity. I could not see the end of sorrow and it felt as if I were sinking slowly toward despair. I told myself that I wasn't worthy to live because I thought that I had already destroyed my own life anyway.

He quickly proved that his apologies were insincere and reenacted the same cycles of abuse. Despite my fragile belief in his apology and will to change, the secret relationship revealed that he was still as abusive and possessive as before. He had lied about his sobriety, and his rage felt more intense than ever. He knew how ashamed I was that we were together, and he threatened to expose me to my friends, my family, and my employers. Every time I expressed my hesitations about our relationship he hurled slurs against me and showed up at my place of work if I didn't answer his calls. I told nobody about our secret relationship because my friends knew the harm that he had caused, and I was terrified that they would hate me for returning to our abusive relationship. No matter how hard I tried to justify my choices, my intuition kept pleading with me to stop. I was ashamed of him, but I was even more ashamed of myself.

It felt like it could not get any worse, and I spent all those months writhing in self-hatred. I told myself that I deserved the abuse because I had actively returned to it, though I must remember that I did not return to him hoping or expecting that he would hurt me again. I was in denial when I reentered our relationship, and I convinced myself that his apologies were sincere. It is difficult for me to articulate these truths because I am aware that while many survivors do everything they can to get away from their abusers, I returned to him. While I am aware that I turned away from my intuition and my friends, I am also aware that he deeply manipulated me into getting back together. Both truths coexist, and his abuse will always remain unacceptable. It is extremely dangerous for survivors to blame ourselves for the violence that we experience. No matter what circumstances we were faced with, none of us deserved to be abused in any way. I do not think that shame and self-hatred assist in healing, and I want to explore with openness, honesty, and self-forgiveness what lived within me that led me back to him.

The possibility of "closure" between us was a myth. We could not arrive at a unified decision to split, and so we spiraled into an agonizing on-again, off-again relationship. We were both so addicted to the chaotic rhythms of our togetherness that neither of us had the willpower to fully separate. I told myself that I needed to see him for the sake of "closure," and the finality I was seeking would be in our next conversation or meeting. I sought closure from him, knowing deep down that his intentions were always aligned to his possessive needs. Every time he was violent with me should have been closure enough, though I later had to unearth the truth that I was resisting the true closure of our union. To find true spiritual closure, I needed to spend time far away from him. I needed to look within.

How have we been taught to mourn? How in our modern world have we been offered support for the funerals we attend and the tears that we must shed? It is simply not enough to be told "Don't cry, just be positive" and "He's trash, don't let his negative energy affect you." Much of the advice we have been taught to give and receive reduces the depths of grief to shallow waters. Despite their good intentions, these responses normalize a careless dismissal of the profoundness of our feelings, even when we are mourning the inevitability of death or separation. I did not provide myself the time to mourn X without judgment because I did not know that I needed to. When I saw him again, it felt as if the ghost of our relationship could still be revived because neither of us had allowed it to die.

We have been taught that funerals are silent and solemn affairs. We are told that public displays of emotion are shameful sights to see. Colonization shaped the modern Western funeral, which usually does not give adequate space to the expansiveness of grief. I have been in mourning spaces that dismissed heightened emotional states as hysteria. I have witnessed how structures of patriarchy have taught men to be afraid of and embarrassed by their tears. In *Ritual*, spiritual teacher Malidoma Patrice Somé writes that "a non-Westerner arriving in this country [America] for the first time is struck by how little attention is given to human emotions in general. People appear to pride themselves for not showing how they feel about anything." We should be allowed and encouraged to grieve at whatever volume and velocity we wish.

In *The Smell of Rain on Dust*, Martín Prechtel writes that tears actively help guide the souls of our loved ones toward peaceful passing. If they are not properly mourned, their souls will linger and haunt the human realm. Prechtel writes that mourning aloud ushers the souls of our loved ones to return to the "Beach of Stars." He taught me that expressive mourning allows the transcendence of our loved ones' spirits. We should be able to cry, thrash, and dance to our heart's content during our ceremonies of grief. We should also be able to move in whatever way feels right with our spirits, so that we can communicate with our loved ones and send them on a safe voyage home.

In the age of technological surveillance, perhaps we think that somebody is always watching us in disapproval. Even in our solitude, we cannot experience our grief at its fullest without feeling policed and surveilled. In moments when I am about to weep, I have found myself looking over my shoulder with deep discomfort and embarrassment. I do not want my grief to slow me down, which I have learned is programming embedded with capitalist intentions. Grieving takes an immense amount of time, and the slowness of grief challenges the fast pace of hyper-individualism. We must be daring enough to patiently move with it together.

When we are told by mass media and surveillance technology to dismiss our grief by engaging in consumptive distractions, we are also being told to look away from the source of our grief. Most of us have experienced immense heartache, but there is certain heartache that some of us should not have had to feel; for example, when we lose our loved ones early due to state-sanctioned abuse that is racist, transphobic, ableist, colorist, and classist. Domestic violence is a direct result of patriarchal hierarchies and supremacy, which parallels the violence of war and genocide. All these forms of abuse require people to be violent to maintain positions of control. In *The Will to Change*, bell hooks wrote extensively about the dominator culture that demands "psychic self-mutilation" to sustain itself and kill off our emotions. When we are told to "not be sad," we are also being ordered to look away from what is required for change. Supporting one another in vital periods of grief can allow us to act toward revolution.

We must move toward an understanding that grief requires nonjudgmental support. We can swim in our grief without completely drowning in it by believing that we can carry one another up from those waters. Support looks like honesty, communication, boundaries, safety, and respect, and it is imperative that we do not resort to shaming survivors for their complicated emotions. Looking back, I realized that I had friends who supported me by telling me that X was dangerous. At the same time, I had acquaintances who would shame me for feeling sad about the dissolution of our relationship. For survivors, receiving support can be just as difficult as asking for it, and we require immense compassion and patience to get there. Receiving compassion can allow survivors to become compassionate with themselves.

I eventually did find support through organizations such as the Anti-Violence Project. Group therapy with the Anti-Violence Project was helpful because it allowed me to feel connected to fellow survivors. We were able to observe one another's coping mechanisms and habits without judgment or shame, which allowed us to vocalize so many things that we were once ashamed of. I have always had a very difficult time crying in front of anybody, and group therapy expanded my capacity to be vulnerable in public. These resources allowed me to see that my grief needed my attention, and that I deserved to be held in that process. It also showed me that mental health support for survivors, especially survivors who do not have health insurance, citizenship, or wealth, needs to be free, encouraged, and readily accessible for us all. Mental health support* can no longer be regarded as a niche avenue of psychology and needs to be mainstreamed as part of a public conversation.

My therapist taught me about the sacred concept of both/and, and how grief can hold many complicated feelings at once. Both/and is the idea that multiple truths can coexist. She never judged or shamed me for my complicated emotions, and even encouraged me to verbalize how much I missed X. She told me that missing him *and* being angry with him were both natural parts of my grief. We can love our parents and resent them at the same time. We can

---

*Resources for mental health and grief support are compiled at the end of this book.

grieve our past relationships and be relieved that they are over. We can pursue joy and still act in self-destructive ways. She told me that whenever I missed him, I needed to express that yearning to her, a friend, or my journal because it would allow me a form of release. She taught me that missing him was not a dedication of energy toward him, but the vital release of energy for me. Most important, she told me not to go to him when I was feeling vulnerable. I learned from her that love never dies, and that my greatest challenge was to locate it within me.

When I was a teenager, I attended my po po's (grandmother's) funeral in Hong Kong. It was a traditional Buddhist ceremony held in a temple, and my extended maternal family had all come to pay their respects. As part of the sacred ritual, we prayed and chanted for nine hours to usher my po po's spirit to the afterlife. Several monks guided our chants while we were kneeling, standing still, or walking in circles. It was pivotal to chant out loud so that her spirit could hear us, and the louder and more repetitive we were, the better. We had to commit to the melodies of the chant so that our message of grievance was clear. Her spirit needed to hear our grief so she could travel safely.

I noticed that with repetition, the chants began to envelop my body. They allowed a vital energy to be released from my soul, an energy that had long been constricted in my chest. During the lengthy ceremony, some of us wept in between chants, some of us chanted loudly then softly, and some of us needed moments of silence. There was no judgment, no hushing, and there was always immense respect. It dawned on me while I was chanting that this was the first major death I had experienced. I realized that the purpose of chanting was not only to usher my grandmother peacefully into the afterlife, but also to release our grief into the ether. It gave us a safe space to express how much we missed her and loved her.

The next day, our family shared a meal together. I remember sitting at a round table opposite my gong gong, my po po's husband, with at least fifteen of my relatives. We were sharing food and conversation and eating our favorite dim sum dishes. I looked up from my bowl and noticed that there were tears streaming down my gong gong's face. He did not say a word, but he also did not stop his tears from flowing. He just sat there eating, sitting with the foods that he'd shared so many times with his wife and his children, and cried. His tears did not make anybody at the table uncomfortable, and I do not think they made him uncomfortable either. After a while, I gave him a hug and began to cry as well. We did not say anything to each other and just allowed this moment to unfold. Our grief was connected as we held each other through it. I learned so much about grief that day.

How do we mourn the relationships that we have lost with people who are living? I have heard many friends describe breakups as a kind of death. X had not died, but our relationship was long deceased despite our toxic efforts to revive it. Our relationship had a soul of its own.

Sometime after the rekindled relationship ended, I performed a long overdue funeral for the soul of our lost love. On small pieces of paper, I wrote every slur he had ever called me that was etched into my mind. This was an extremely painful practice, because I had to recall so many of the vulgarities that still lived within me. Each time I wrote something down, it felt like an extraction of poison. Looking at these slurs on paper allowed me to see that they were not inherent parts of me but lived outside of me. They were projections used to invoke fear in my spirit, and at the same time were reflections of the fear that lived in X's heart. Twenty scattered pieces of paper surrounded me in a circle, and I read each of them out loud, burning them one by one. I cried as I read them, and I felt myself missing him too. This was a ritual of release. I watched them turn into ashes and realized that I was initiating a long overdue funeral service of my own. I allowed myself to weep as loudly as I needed to. I wept about the pain, the violence, the abuse, and for the first time in a long time, I wept for me.

The funeral for our relationship helped me to express all my complicated emotions in an alleviating synthesis. In that moment, I no longer compartmentalized my feelings in binaries of good or bad. I stopped chasing utopias and allowed myself to steep in the depths of my grief. I let all the nuanced feelings that were held in both/and to come together and coexist. I finally gave myself permission to miss him as all the joyful, loving, painful, and violent memories played out before me. I wept and sobbed and lamented out loud, sending the lost soul of our love affair to the afterlife. Grieving my life without him meant that I had to usher in a new life. The ceremony simultaneously honored the death of our relationship and celebrated a new mysterious beginning that awaited me.

I do not believe that grief ever disappears. Grief morphs and shape-shifts as we honor it, as it begins to entwine with the contours of love. At times, it can tug at your heart and break it, especially on days when you feel vulnerable and tender. On other days, it can fill your spirit with immense gratitude for a life that was shared and a life that continues. In the *Tibetan Book of the Dead*, I learned that death is not an ending but a transfer of energy. As our tears send spirits to the afterlife, their energy is transmuted to new life. Our grief transforms, too, into an energy of love.

When I finally grieved my relationship with X, I was able to acknowledge that my capacity for tenderness did not die along with our union; I just needed it to be redirected toward myself. I grieved our relationship to make space for new possibilities of true love. When I grieved my po po, I deeply appreciated her life and my own, and I watched the seeds she planted blossom into illuminating seedlings of her legacy. Each time I have explored the murky waters of grief, I have become profoundly closer to myself. To this day, grief has shown me that love does not die at the face of death; it is transformed. Our funerals are commemorations of life, and they honor what needs to be released. When you grieve deeply, you are shown your abounding capacity to love. Love does not die. Love sprouts from the ground that we have nourished with our tears.

FIVE

DISTRUST

Trusting Ourselves in Change

Trigger Warning: Sexual Violence and Abuse

Every morning, a delicate iridescent hummingbird hovers outside my window. His arrival feels like a blessed omen and a message of love. I always greet him as he rapidly beats his wings, and I wonder if he ever gets tired of movement. Some days, I try to take it a step further and open the window, but every time he buzzes away and disappears out of sight. He always comes back the next day, drinking the nectar from the marigolds on my windowsill, and I observe his flight with admiration. It is clear to me that my sudden movements are perceived by him as a threat, and that it will take him some time to trust me. Lately, I open the window a little slower, and I find that he is not as quick to fly away. He watches me for a second, less scared but more inquisitive, and then he flutters away. As he takes flight once more, I watch his beating wings, acknowledging that he hums for his survival. I hope that he lands in a quiet place to rest once his belly is full of the sweet gold nectar.

All living beings have adapted many ways of sensing danger. I think of the beings I grew up with: observant stray cats, green tree frogs, towering prickly succulents, and shy mimosa plants. Like our plant and animal kin, we display learned and intuitive biological reactions to what we perceive as threatening to our safety and well-being. Most of us who have experienced trauma can be hypervigilant and hold distrust in our hearts, and our bodies can often react in a multitude of learned and innate ways. Our protective tendencies show just how much we value our lives.

Neither survival nor danger is new to Earth, though some human beings seem to be responsible for the invention of new threats. The new challenges we face make us question whether we still know how to distinguish safety from danger. What happens when love presents itself to us and we perceive it as a threat? What happens when danger is nearby, and we perceive it as love?

Somatic healing practitioners have distinguished the most common survival strategies as **flight**, **fight**, **freeze**, **appease**, and **dissociate**. In *The Politics of Trauma*, Staci K. Haines closely studies the iterations of each reaction, explaining that "these protective responses are well beyond our conscious capacity to control them. We have inherited them through both evolution and the particular biology of who made and birthed us. In turn, they work with the interpersonal, cultural, and social context in which we live."

Even abusive intimate relationships can disguise themselves as love. After we experience abuse, it becomes increasingly difficult for us to identify who we can trust. Close relationships can feel like threats to our safety. When abuse has been enacted in romantic, platonic, or familial relationships, it can feel either risky or "boring" to experience true love in comparison with previous toxic relationships. My survival mechanisms would always flare up when I made new connections. I have found myself fearful, hypervigilant, and stubbornly detached. I did not trust myself, let alone anybody else. This has led me to explore my survival strategies and unpack the past trauma I was responding to. Understanding this forced me to look at the violence that has historically, personally, and systemically been normalized in association with "love." It has taken me a long time to understand that I was not afraid of love. Instead, I was fearful of the abuse that has disguised itself as love.

I have witnessed violence seep into intimate relationships, and I have seen how love has been misconstrued as the means to abuse, control, and possess. I have witnessed love disguised as "passion" and rewritten as domination. There is so much to heal from that requires us to embark on a continuing unpacking of systemic violence, hierarchical supremacy, gender roles, and childhood traumas. With so much to unlearn, how can we come closer to trusting one another? First, we can listen to our intuitions and tend to our various survival mechanisms to understand what makes us feel safe. Our survival mechanisms are unique, brilliant, and necessary, and they can tell us a lot about what we care about, what we fear, and what can bring us closer to love.

I think of the hummingbird that hums before me, and how each day we seem to become closer in trust. I consider my own bodily instincts, and how my biological and psychological survival mechanisms endeavor to protect me. Not only are they telling me how to react to dangerous situations, but they are also affirming that I am deserving of abundance and safety. Instead of pointing a trembling finger at love, I look closely and gently at my fear. I see that there is plenty of room to relearn trust and closeness. Funnily enough, love is the force that guides me through. Love is what allows us to survive.

One night, I decided to end my rekindled abusive relationship with X once and for all. We had just eaten a secret meal together and were decompressing in bed. I was quiet all night, nervously conjuring my words. I felt depleted, fragmented, and heartbroken beyond belief. Every time we slept together, it felt like I was tearing myself apart. I was afraid of how he would retaliate after hearing this abrupt news, so I decided to tell him that I needed to step away from our sexual relationship. It would be the first step in our detachment. I muttered, "I think we should stop sleeping together."

He was enraged by my suggestion and got up, alarmed. He stared at me in disbelief and exclaimed, "Why? Are you sleeping with someone else?!" I shook my head and closed my eyes, already drained by his accusation. It was the same manipulative tactic he always used to make me feel like the villain. I replied in frustration, "No! Our relationship is unhealthy, and I don't think we should sleep together anymore. It fucks everything up and is the main reason we keep coming back!" He winced in rage and started yelling obscenities about me being a slut who discarded him as soon as I found someone better. He yelled, "I know that you're fucking someone else! Keep looking because nobody's ever going to love you! Nobody's ever going to love you when I'm done with you."

I will not, and quite frankly cannot, describe what physically happened next because my body and mind had shut down. When I later described what had happened to a friend, they told me that I was raped. It takes immense courage to even utter that word. Describing the violence felt abhorrent because my most common survival strategy was dissociation. All I can recall with clarity is the initial resistance: the kicking, the screaming, and the attempt to push him away. I remember sobbing and begging him to stop, and I remember how he continued to violate me anyway. After that, nothing. Everything went blank. I felt like I was looking away from outside of my body, as if my spirit had departed and drifted away. As soon as it was over, I could not shed a single tear. This was the day I got to know the kind of grief that asked me to mourn parts of myself that had been taken. He had stolen my agency, my body, and my relationship with desire. He had used my body as a vessel for his pleasure—not just for his sexual desire, but for his insecure need to control me and keep me close. After he was done, it felt like I no longer had a body. After he was done, it felt like I was nothing at all.

Staci K. Haines offers the closest description of my aftermath in *The Politics of Trauma*, where she uses a term I had never heard before, "traumatic amnesia," which is essentially a deeper extension of dissociation. She explains by writing,

> Sometimes we will just not remember the feelings of the experience: "I was raped, it wasn't a big deal. I'm over it." Or, we don't register the experience as we would a regular memory. Then, we do not remember the experience(s) mentally, or in our self-concept. We do, however, remember them in our tissues, emotions, and survival reactions.

My traumatic amnesia lasted for a long time and drove me to a place of deep shame. I had shut down, and I did not feel safe verbalizing my outrage, concern, or sorrow, because that would require me to admit that the rape happened. I fell asleep soon after and said nothing when I woke up next to him the following day.

One week later, X went to a psychiatrist and started taking anxiety and anger-management medication. We never addressed the rape, though it lingered in the back of my mind. He told me that he was seeking immediate help. I was lost in despair and felt completely dissociated from my body. I was no longer present in the relationship or with myself. Whenever he wanted to see me, I obliged. Whatever he wanted me to do, I obeyed. I put my self-destruction in his hands because I already felt destroyed and beyond support or healing. I started to blame myself for the rape and no longer trusted my own instincts. One day, he was extremely calm after taking his pills and asked me how I was doing. My dissociation came to an abrupt halt, and it felt like I had snapped back into a sharp static reality. I was in fight mode. My body remembered, and my recollections came back to me with this unexpected trigger. For a clarifying moment, I was back in my body, and I was disgusted and enraged.

I started screaming at him for having the nerve to ask me how I was: "How dare you ask me that?! You know exactly how I am! You get all the help in the world, you get meds and friends who enable your abuse, and what do I have? You destroyed me! You raped me, beat me, emotionally abused me! I am disgusted by you, and I hate you and I hate myself because of you!"

He turned toward me, shook his head, and said, "You have a problem. I don't know why you're so angry." Then he walked out the door. I never saw him again.

Staci K. Haines introduced me to somatic healing, which suggests that the body, spirit, and mind are all connected in recovery. Somatic healing requires us to tend to our mental health triggers, reactions, and coping mechanisms to then connect us to PTSD-centered physical therapy so that we can learn new healthy patterns. It can include mindfulness practices, grounding techniques, talk therapy, and body movement work. Somatic healing practitioners describe the interconnected body, spirit, and mind as the "somatic body," which is also known as the "soma." Haines describes our somatic beings as "a combination of biological, evolutionary, emotional, and psychological aspects, shaped by social and historical norms, and adaptive to a wide array of both resilient and oppressive forces." Somatic healing requires us to see that every part of our healing is connected.

Haines explores somatic healing practices as a framework that beckons us to ask deeper questions about our trauma.

Much of the current research is focused around the use of somatics in healing trauma, at which it is very effective. But the question of why there is so much trauma and oppression to heal and what somatics can do about it, is often left unasked. While somatics has much to offer in healing, a somatic approach without an analysis of social and economic institutions, unequal distribution of power, and use of violence and coercion, excludes some of the largest forces that shape us.

While we collectively uncover our individual pain and traumas, we must also ask why we are experiencing them in the first place. As a survivor of intimate partner violence, I witnessed instances of domination, racial misogyny, patriarchy, and fetishization in my relationship with X. Zooming out, I saw how they were all connected to the gendered systems of violence, fascism, racism, and xenophobia that rule our modern world. So many of us have been personally manipulated into thinking that violence goes hand in hand with love. No wonder we are fearful of "love" and find it extremely difficult to trust one another.

Both X and I are children of immigrants of color. I was raised as a woman, and he was raised as a man. It is important to note these specific identities within our relationship because it allows me to name one of the major factors in our abusive dynamic: patriarchal supremacy. When Staci K. Haines prompts us to think not only about our traumas but also about *why* we keep getting traumatized in the first place, it allows me to trace intimate partner violence back to points that are inseparable from patriarchy, toxic masculinity, misogyny, colonization, racism, white supremacy, and domination. I investigate this wider framework not to excuse X, but to look at the root of the violence and investigate what urgently needs to change.

The prolific bell hooks taught me that love and violence simply cannot coexist. She wrote many books about her personal, communal, and systemic encounters with love alongside patriarchal systems of oppression. Her work vulnerably unpacks her personal trauma as a Black woman who navigated close relationships with men, while also dissecting the many layers of systemic abuse she faced as a Black woman living in America. In her book *The Will to Change*, she wrote that "passive male absorption of sexist ideology enables men to falsely interpret this disturbed behavior positively.

As long as men are brainwashed to equate violent domination and abuse of women with privilege, they will have no understanding of the damage done to themselves or to others, and no motivation to change."

It requires immense compassion (that I have not always had the capacity for) to see why the abusers in intimate relationships are so often (but not always) cisgender men. Initially I was resistant to it, telling myself that I could care less to learn about the sources of patriarchal violence; all I knew was that it needed to stop. However, I later realized that by extending that compassion toward men I was inadvertently extending compassion toward myself, because it provided me with hope that there was possibility for change. As much as I try to deny it, I will always have an attachment to men, whether through family, work, friendship, or romance. I have brothers, a father, paternal figures, and friends whom I deeply care for and wish to hold accountable. We must exist among men, and spending our days living in fear is not ideal for our survival. Cisgender men must be determined to release their "privilege" to reduce harm and violence in this world. Men need to heal.

Patriarchal supremacy does not wholly benefit anybody. While systemically, white cisgender men typically benefit from having more access to wealth, career opportunities, health care, and (stolen) land, their privileges are emotionally and spiritually barren. While men who enact patriarchal supremacy feed off the "power" of domination, they also become emotionally devoid and isolated. I have met cisgender men of all races and sexualities who have told me that they have not cried in more than a decade. This doesn't seem to be because men are biologically incapable of feeling emotions, but because they have been taught since birth, by caregivers who had to survive within patriarchal systems, that their emotions were invalid. When one's worth, since childhood, is determined by measures of "power," then one's actions will unravel into a pattern of domination and control.

In *The Will to Change*, bell hooks talked about how these patterns manifest in intimate relationships: "Within a culture of domination struggles for power are enacted daily in human relationships, often assuming their worst forms in situations of intimacy." As gendered binaries reinstate emotions as inherently feminine, toxic masculinity asks men to flee from their feelings and to run toward mythical and emotionless ideals. How can cisgender men understand what it means to be loving in close relationships, when they have been taught that closeness, intimacy, emotions, and love make them "weak"? Cisgender men are not even taught to be close to themselves.

Ocean Vuong poignantly talked about the intertwining natures of violence and toxic masculinity in an interview with Seth Meyers.*

In this culture, we celebrate boys through the lexicon of violence. "You're killing it." "You're making a killing." "Smash 'em." "Blow 'em up." "You went into that game guns blazing." And I think it's worth it to ask the question: What happens to our men and boys when the only way they can valuate themselves is through the lexicon of death and destruction? And I think that when they see themselves only worthwhile when they're capable of destroying things it's inevitable that we arrive at a masculinity that is toxic.

---

*You can watch an excerpt of the interview on YouTube: youtube.com /watch?v=cQl_qbWwCwU&t=162s.

Men of color can partake in the same systems of domination, because it provides an illusion of "power." That "power" is usually wielded at the detriment of others, especially toward people who are not men. People who are not men can also participate in systems of patriarchal thinking, because most of us were raised to believe that was the norm. I had to unlearn ample internalized misogyny, which usually manifested itself as jealousy and competition with women and anyone feminine-presenting so that I could gain patriarchal respect or validation. People who hold on to toxic masculinity and patriarchal supremacy as a means of protection require deep practices of unlearning too. Patriarchal supremacy cannot take the shape of love because its shapes are morphed from violence.

In the speech "The Master's Tools Will Never Dismantle the Master's House,"* Audre Lorde critiques white feminism and its tendencies to adapt racist and patriarchal hierarchies: "Women of today are still being called upon to stretch across the gap of male ignorance and to educate men as to our existence and our needs. This is an old and primary tool of all oppressors to keep the oppressed occupied with the master's concerns." While it is not my responsibility to do the work for cisgender men, I can only hope that they actively do the work to dismantle these spiritually barren structures of domination. I hope that all of us can unlearn the poisonous tenets of toxic masculinity and ensure that domination does not equate to love.

Staci K. Haines describes supremacist systems as "power-over systems": "Power-over economic, political, and social systems concentrate safety, belonging, dignity, decision making, and resources

---

*You can read this speech in Audre Lorde's collection of essays and speeches *Sister Outsider*.

within a few elite, and particular nation-states. This is done by taking from and exploiting others in the natural world. Those who
are harmed and made poor are blamed in broader social narratives." Anything built on violence and the harming of others is not
inherently loving or "powerful." The most powerful thing we can
do is envision loving and equitable futures that heal the wounds
left in all of us.

A scarcity mindset inflames the distrust of the world's majority
because resources have been hoarded by an exclusive "elite." We
want to hold on to privileges because we think that they will ensure
our safety, dignity, and joy. But what happens when those privileges
hurt others? Abusive partners, who may be survivors themselves,
usually cause harm to exert control over their significant others and
keep them by their side, reclaiming a sense of "power" that might
have been taken from them by society, by their workplace, or by the
circumstances of their childhood. In *The End of Manhood*, which bell
hooks quotes in *Killing Rage*, John Stoltenberg offers this advice to
men who are trying to release these ideas of "power": "Learning to
live as a man of conscience means deciding that your loyalty to the
people whom you love is always more important than whatever lingering loyalty you may sometimes feel to other men's judgment on
your manhood." If we are committed to ending sexual abuse, intimate partner violence, police brutality, and war, then we must be
willing to critically analyze the harmful ideas of masculinity, hierarchy, and power that we have inherited since birth.

What are we willing to give up so that we can ensure safety,
healing, liberation, and love for all? This is a question for anybody
who finds themselves wrestling with internalized patriarchy and
masculinity, and it unravels into a deeper question: Who can I be
without these systems of domination and illusions of power? We

have always been wholly capable of loving, and healing looks like returning to our deepest interconnected selves, prior to power-over programming. You do not need to be dependent on adapting power-over behaviors to feel worthy of being alive. You do not have to deem others unworthy to enhance your own miraculous life.

People who have enacted any form of harm must be willing to release these illusions of domination and truly reflect on what that false sense of power is built on. Cisgender men must be willing to shed themselves of toxic masculinity and the violence that leaches on to it. For them to heal, they must be willing to feel. Otherwise, they will continue to replicate patterns of abuse. In Audre Lorde's aforementioned seminal speech, she said, "For the master's tools will never dismantle the master's house. They may allow us temporarily to beat him at his own game, but they will never enable us to bring about genuine change." We need to unlearn the patriarchal game and burn the house to the ground.

Time and again I have mistaken desire for love. I cannot talk about desire without talking about how specific social programming has shaped and defined desirability. Western and Eurocentric standards of desire have affected how people have pursued me and, most jarringly, how I see myself. I have even been told to be grateful for that obtuse desire, even when it is built on racist misogynistic assumptions. Their idealizations reduce me to an ornament and make me feel like an accessory to a person's hunt for control. My experiences with intimate partner violence are deeply connected to racist desirability programming because X's ability to harm me was entwined with his flattening projections of my Asian heritage and femininity. His actions were connected to acts of racist misogynistic violence that have been committed against women and femmes of color, some of whom have survived, and some who have not.

On March 16, 2021, in Atlanta, Georgia, a white supremacist man went on a rampage at three different massage parlors and shot and killed eight people, six of them Asian (Chinese and Korean) women.* Countless ignorant articles appeared on news platforms speculating his motives and openly debating whether the killings were "racially motivated." The massacre happened during a surge of violent attacks on Asian elders in America, which was a result of fascist propaganda that deemed China (and therefore all Chinese and "Chinese-looking" people) as the villain responsible for the COVID-19 pandemic. As mainstream media questioned the intentions and mental health of the murderer without examining his white supremacist intentions, both Asian and Asian American communities and our allies were outraged by the blatant denial of another mass shooting fueled by white supremacy.

After the killings, there was much speculation that the murderer had a sex addiction and questions were raised about whether the women he targeted were sex workers whom he blamed for his sexual shame. Red Canary Song,† an organization that works with

---

*It is important to specify hyphenated identities, but I use the term "Asian" here because I do not know whether they identified as Asian or Asian American, though I do know that they were first-generation immigrants.

†Check out their extremely important work at redcanarysong.net.

migrant and Asian sex workers in New York City, released a statement in response to the incident that said in part, "Whether or not
they were actually sex workers or self-identified under that label,
we know that as massage workers, they were subjected to sexualized violence stemming from the hatred of sex workers, Asian
women, working class people, and immigrants." Furthermore, no
protection is offered to sex workers (especially sex workers of
color), migrant workers, women (especially trans women), and nonbinary people of color. White supremacy fantasizes Asian women
and femmes as subservient, demure, obedient, delicate, and silent,
and therefore available for abuse and domination. These fantasies
are a direct result of revolting historical Western propaganda that
marches in lockstep with waging war, fascism, xenophobia, and
anti-Blackness. A white man killed eight living, breathing human
beings that day to stifle his self-hatred and shame, while carrying
out the very same violent intentions that America's white supremacist systems were built on.

When I heard about the shooting, I was seething, terrified, and
distraught. I cried for days and spiraled into a deep depression and
anger, every hair on my body standing on high alert. For some reason, I could not stop thinking about my dating history and all the
times I had been targeted by fetishistic men. A survival strategy
that rarely ever awakens was triggered: the instinct to fight. My
urge to fight came from a decade of unprocessed hurt that all
seemed to be flooding rapidly toward me. I started to recall men
who tried to follow me home as a child, men who catcalled at me
using racial slurs, and even ex-lovers who I knew only wanted to
date me to fulfill their anime girl fetishes. X had a known Asian fetish and had dated many Asian women before me, which was another layer to his violence that I had always been reluctant to

unpack. His perceptions of my Asian femininity made it easy for him to abuse me. After the shooting, I was once again fearful for my survival in ways that felt all too familiar. It is a fear that I will never forget.

"Ornamentalism" is a term that combines "ornamental" and "Orientalism." It is also the title of a book by theorist Anne Anlin Cheng that explores the idea that ornamentalism is the "conceptual framework for approaching a history of racialized person-making, not through biology but through synthetic inventions and ornamentations." As a Chinese American woman, she studied how "yellow" women* have historically been reduced to less than human fragmentations and morphed by the threatened Western imagination into delicate, decorative objects.

> Encrusted by representations, abstracted and reified, the yellow woman is persistently sexualized yet barred from sexuality, simultaneously made and unmade by the aesthetic project. Like the proverbial Ming vase, she is at once ethereal and base, an object of value and a hackneyed trope.

Ornamentalism contains historical photographs and paintings of Chinese women that were captured by white men. Shown next to vases and flowers, most of these women usually blend into the background. Cheng traces the roots of ornamentalism and fetishization, and acknowledges that they are not exclusive to "yellow" women.

---

*When she writes "yellow women," she is referring to East Asian and East Asian–presenting women. In *Ornamentalism*, she specifically explores European men's historical representations of Chinese women.

She leads us back to the historical and sexualized violence that was (and still is) committed against Black women.

> Our models for understanding racialized gender have been predominantly influenced by a particular view of bodies of African origins that has led us to think in a certain way about raced female bodies, when there has been in fact something of a bifurcation within the racial imaginary between bare flesh and artificial ornament. These two aesthetic vocabularies are clearly both racialized, but they do *not* necessarily or even primarily index racial identities.

It is clear that the images, portrayals, and ideas of non-white women and femmes have long been controlled in many different ways by white men for their motivations of violence and domination.

In a *New York Times* article titled "The Alt-Right's Asian Fetish,"* journalist Audrea Lim wrote about how alt-right neo-Nazi white supremacists commonly pursue Asian women as their wives. These white men regard white women as too assertive and "feminist," and therefore no longer desirable or aligned with their agendas. They prey on working-class migrant Asian women and promise to be their providers if these women do exactly as they say. Fetishists have a severe power imbalance that services the fulfillment of a constructed white supremacist fantasy. According to them, Asian women, especially Asian women in Asia, are way more malleable than white women and appropriate for "wife material." Lim wrote

---

*You can read this article online at nytimes.com/2018/01/06/opinion/sunday/alt-right-asian-fetish.html.

about her personal reflections and how those ideas affected her own self-esteem growing up.

> This fun-house mirror asks me to be smarter, nicer, prettier and more accomplished than my white counterparts for the same amount of respect, then floods my dating app inbox with messages that reek of Asian fetish. . . . But none of us can escape the truth that the fun-house was built to justify systematic exploitation of everyone in this country who isn't white. That's important context.

The most insidious part of racial misogyny is that it alters the ways we see one another and ourselves. It became apparent to me that the ex-partners who fetishized me did not care for my body, heart, and spirit. All that mattered was that I was beautiful, obedient, and faithful, and as soon as I was not, I was disposable and easily replaced by somebody they deemed easier to control. I have become suspicious, hypercritical, competitive, and jealous of people who look like me because I have perceived them as a threat to my partnerships. I have been dismissive and envious of brilliant, kind, and beautiful Asian and Asian American women, femmes, and nonbinary people whom I have seen as a threat. I acted out in petty ways, instead of being critical of my ex-partners who fetishized all of us in the same ways.

A loving romantic relationship is a mutual union between two (or more) people, and no loving relationship can be nourished if either person is not regarded as human in the first place. Fetishistic desire shatters our connections with one another and ourselves and turns our comrades into threats. We must do the labor of deep unlearning. Love cannot coexist alongside fetish and domination, and we must free ourselves of these fantasies that turn us into vases, shadows, and ghosts. One of the only ways to rebuke these hollow fantasies is to be grounded in community and to relearn what abundant love can truly look like. I want to trust in love, and I can only be in a loving, trusting relationship with somebody who is also willing to sacrifice these illusions of "power," release their learned ideas of fetishistic desirability, and dismantle these structures of domination.

Dating after my relationship with X felt impossible. I trusted no one. Sleeping with people felt "easy" because I was so dissociated after the rape and no longer believed that sex required emotional closeness. Emotionless sex became a short-term distraction from the deep pain that I was harboring inside. I was very promiscuous, though I was always detached from the people I was sleeping with. I no longer knew how to say "no," because my "no" had been violated. My consent did not seem to have any value, so before checking in with my body, I launched into physical relationships with anybody who showed desire for me. However, whenever emotional connection was required, my "no" would become shrill and panic-stricken, and I would immediately abandon the relationship. My integrity and boundaries felt broken, and it was difficult to distinguish my desire from my actions. My true desire was to relearn love and experience it from within, but because I did not know that yet, I only had the capacity to wade in the shallow waters of physical attraction.

I saw a toxic pattern reoccurring fling after fling, and I wanted it to stop. Even though I did not have the language of somatic healing yet, I instinctually began to interrogate my somatic body and the coping mechanisms and survival strategies that my soma often resorted to. I listened to the entwined languages of my body, spirit, and mind and heard them whisper memories into my reactions. I wanted to learn new patterns, and I knew that I needed to break the cycle.

As I referenced at the start of the chapter, the most common survival strategies for our somas are **flight, fight, freeze, appease**, and **dissociate**. Staci K. Haines writes that all our somatic survival strategies are inherently brilliant and ingrained in our systems, and they come from instincts that are also adapted by our animal relatives. I will elaborate on each of these somatic responses as defined by Haines and explain how I have adapted them in my own personal experiences.

Flight is "the impulse and action of getting out of or away from a threatening person, experience, or situation." Every time I blocked and deleted X, I was following my flight impulse because I knew that contact was dangerous. After I was assaulted, locking myself in his bathroom and devising my getaway plan was my flight response in action. Fleeing from X after the assault was essential for my survival, and I am eternally grateful for the ways that my soma advocated for my escape.

However, flight responses can also be "held at a sustained level over time" and "mobilized repeatedly in your soma . . . even though it does not take care of your life and your commitments." For example, after my abusive relationship with X, I found myself hesitant to engage in any close intimate relationships. When people expressed their romantic feelings for me, I "escaped" by saying that they were misreading our relationship, even though I had been sending mixed signals. I would abandon the relationship immediately, no matter how much I liked them, because I did not want to relive the pain that my soma still associated with romance. For a while, flight was my recurrent response to intimate relationships, regardless of whether they were harmful or not. It took time for me to learn that I could be communicative and honest with people who were not trying to hurt me. I could stay if I wanted to.

Fight is "the protective mobilization to threaten, get bigger than, position and defend, and intimidate to ward off or dissipate threat." The fight response does not exclusively refer to physical retaliation but also encompasses strategic acts of resistance to protest abusive people and systems of power. However, much intention, consideration, preparation, and support are required before any action; otherwise, our fight responses may put us in unsafe situations. I rarely fought back at X, though there were times when, at my most enraged, I utilized the sacred breath of my anger and screamed in my defense. My suppressed rage manifested itself as shrill insults and threats, though it was difficult for me to feel safe. As I said before, expressing rage toward an abuser may not be the safest thing for a survivor to do, so I rarely used fight as a survival mechanism. Most of the time, it felt as if I were fighting myself.

Freeze is the "protective mobilization to be deeply still, not move, and wait until it is over." In the face of heightened physical conflict, I tend to freeze and do nothing until it is over. Since childhood, anytime I have been catcalled and yelled at on the street, I rarely react or speak up for myself. I am usually frozen in embarrassment; it takes at least fifteen seconds after the encounter has passed for me to come up with a response. I used to be ashamed of my inability to react, but now I know that it was my soma protecting me from the potential escalation to violence.

Appease is the "protective mobilization to pacify, placate, become smaller than and less threatening, so as to ward off threat or dissipate it." This survival mechanism is extremely familiar to my soma because I was born in predominantly white Australia. My identity as a queer Chinese person heavily informs my survival mechanism to appease. The cultural Chinese practices that my parents and I grew up with usually instilled the need to "save face," which meant to hide our negative emotions in public. This was amplified when we were living in a place where we were the stark minority. My soma activated my appeasing strategies in a range of relationships, from dealing with the power-over dynamics of white bullies in my childhood schools to dealing with X in my adulthood. Often during my abusive relationship, I was willing to appease as an avoidant tactic for de-escalation.

Finally, **dissociation** is "the protective mobilization to get away without physically leaving, to numb awareness and feeling, to check out so as not to be there for whatever is happening. My dissociation was extreme during each assault and every time I was triggered and reminded of them afterward. I would spiritually leave my body and resort to indulgent partying or scrolling aimlessly on my phone to prolong the numbness. I still tend to do this, especially in response to receiving traumatic news, and while I am grateful for the temporary reprieve, I also must remind myself that my healing process requires me to return to the present.

Our survival strategies teach us that there is validity in our distrust, and that our somas are always equipped and ready to protect us. While the first step in relearning trust is trusting ourselves, we must also remember that our somas act according to what is familiar to them. To expand our trust, we must also be open to new familiarities. This is what Staci K. Haines refers to as "somatic opening." We must be open to learning new forms of love, and not allow our fears to impede us in nourishing new relationships, especially the relationships we have with ourselves. Our somas show us that we want to continue living, and that we want to experience the healthiest and most dignifying forms of love and relationships, starting with ourselves. We deserve it.

While I have spent ample time shaming myself for my coping mechanisms, what I have learned about our survival strategies is that they have the capacity for adaptation and change. I am grateful for the ways that I have protected myself in the past, for that tells me that I want to live. It tells me that, even if I do not know it, I cherish my miraculous life. By learning about somatic healing, I have become aware of my somatic reactions, which has deepened my relationship to myself. Now, whatever mode I am in—flight, fight, freeze, appease, or dissociate—there is a speck of awareness that zooms out to the bigger picture. In those precious and brief moments, I can discern whether I am truly facing the threat of danger, or whether I am being triggered by memories from the past. I can do so lovingly and without judgment, as I unlearn toxic familiarities and expand myself for new possibilities. Building a trusting relationship with myself allowed me to no longer mistake domination, violence, or control for love. Love cannot coexist with violence, and somatic healing encourages me to remember that.

What is survival if not the fight for loving continuance? The beauty of somatic healing is that it allows us to create new patterns while distinguishing which ones feel familiar to our bodies. Upon becoming aware of my survival strategies, I decided to take some time away from dating to become open to new sensations of trust in my body. I focused my attention on nourishing relationships with my friends and family that were not romantic partnerships. This was not a means to avoid romantic partnerships, but a generative and open space for me to nourish a trusting relationship with myself. I took that time to discern what I truly wanted in an intimate partnership and how I deserved to be treated.

I rediscovered trust by reading books by myself, writing without self-judgment in my journal every day, and going on long walks accompanied by trees, bees, and flowers. I slowly and courageously got closer to people and opened up to them about my most vulnerable experiences and emotions. Through fostering non-romantic relationships with my friends, human and nonhuman alike, I learned that closeness takes trust, nourishment, and openness. My soma was relearning new patterns of closeness, shedding fearful projections, showing immense gratitude, and blossoming open for love.

During the first year of the pandemic, in 2020, I lost my grandfather. I had grown up with him in a home that I had been unable to return to (for immigration reasons) for three years. When I learned of his ascension, I was incapable of processing the loss of this wonderful man. I was distraught and in denial for a very long time. Eventually, six months after his passing, I sat down to write in my journal while listening to Franz Liszt's Consolation no. 3 and his spirit came to me. My grandfather had introduced me to classical music and always sat with me while I played the piano as a child. My grandfather taught me that playing music was about feeling, not perfection. He taught me to trust my emotions, to believe in my imagination, and to explore my mistakes. It was my grandfather who taught me that it is possible for a man to be in touch with his emotions and be thoroughly committed to anti-misogyny and anti-racism. He taught me that there are so many possibilities beyond the toxic bounds that have been drawn up for us, and that my heart must stay open to them. Even in his ascension, he showed me that it is possible to imagine new futures of trust.

As I wept about how much I missed him, I reflected on the lessons of trust he often shared. I was grieving because my love was so deep, and I was moved because his presence in my life showed me that loving and trusting relationships are possible and require work. He was a man who never shed his curiosity, stayed open to the world, and was not afraid to cry. When my parents were working tirelessly to pay the bills, he held my hand and walked me to school. On those walks, he was always immensely present with me, and he showed me bees dancing in pollen, pointed out the way that bark peels off paperbark trees, and whistled along with the birds. Sometimes when I go on walks, I picture him walking with me.

The grief often rises through my soma, and often my somatic reaction is to sit in stillness with his spirit. His energy has shifted, and it has a home with me. As I was journaling and listening to the tinkling sounds of Liszt's composition, I felt a warmth cradle my body, and I looked outside my window to see the hummingbird hovering again. My grandfather was still with me everywhere: in the budding roses, the butterflies, and the hummingbird's beating wings. He was with me in every moment of closeness, teaching me new blossoming possibilities of love and trust.

SIX

SHAME

Getting to Know Our Ghosts

W e live in a world of hauntings. Our ghosts surround us in shimmering swirls, and sometimes in the darkness of the night, or when a breeze blows during the heat of the summer, I feel the chill of my ghosts when they glide through my body. I have tried to return to an "untainted" version of myself, one that was oblivious to the visceral natures of pain and loss. I obsess over an imagined place of "purity," where the ghosts of my past do not roam, and I realize that as vital as it is to release my hauntings, I cannot return to a self who is untouched by pain. I do not live in a world without pain, and I cannot pretend that pain does not continue as I continue too.

I once thought of my healing as a return to "innocent" versions of myself. I tried for many years to outrun my hauntings and shed the chilling cloak of ghosts that followed me around. When I found myself incapable of doing so, a shame festered in my body, taking residence in my chest and my throat. I would blame myself for not being completely "healed" and for not having the strength to "overcome." My shame did not help my healing, and my punitive attitudes did not create space for accountability. My ghosts remained.

Can we think of our ghosts as guides? Especially when they visit us when we least expect them? Our hauntings linger for their very own reasons, and as painful as it can be to sit with them, it can be generative to understand what our ghosts are trying to tell us. They ignite conversations within us with our ancestors, our elders, our children, and they create space for us to let go. An ethic of punishment runs deep in our racist ruling systems and infiltrates the education we receive as children. We are taught to categorize ourselves as either good/bad, pure/broken, hero/villain, when none of those categories honor the fullness of our complexities. You may have heard of the film *The Good, the Bad and the Ugly*, in which the word "ugly" adds another dimension to the binary of good and evil. Perhaps there is an abundance of knowledge within these "ugly"* spaces that we try to avoid. In my healing, I am devoted to shedding light on the unpalatable feelings that I was taught to be ashamed of. These spaces are not pure; they are messy, complicated, hurtful, healing, and changing. The more we ostracize them, the more shame is created within us.

Stewing in shame is a trap that halts possibilities for change, healing, and accountability. Yearning for an "untainted" past

---

*When I say "ugly," I mean unpalatable to mainstream society.

ignores the survival that shaped us. Most of us have experienced harm, and there is no perfect person who is exempt from causing harm either. Perhaps you know the phrase "Hurt people hurt people." It is true, but we need to expand upon this sentence. How do we heal hurt people so we can commit to not harming people (including ourselves) anymore? How can we use accountability to transform our behaviors while also diffusing the stickiness of shame? Shame is a feeling of perpetual regret, and it holds us hostage to fruitless wishes of undoing. Only when we really get to know our hauntings can we release shame and enact change. We need to move from a place of possibility instead of punishment. We need to believe that we deserve better and can do better. Though we were not deserving of our hurt, we are deserving of transformative continuance. Our hauntings teach us that although we may be incapable of reversal, we are capable of infinite transformation.

I will never return to a pre-abused place, which is a hard pill to swallow. That place no longer exists and striving to get there was a disservice to the hardships I have endured. I fragmented myself by putting myself in categories of "pre" and "post" abuse. It created a harmful binary within me that labeled me "whole" before the abuse and "broken" afterward. It hindered me from seeing myself as a synthesis of past, present, and future. If I perpetually wished for the self that existed before the assault, then I was also not accepting who I was in the present. Even if I were to trace my self back to before the assault, I would not be pure or free from harm. It has taken me a long time to feel at home with all my culminating realities. My new home holds both the painful lessons that I learned and the divine love that allowed me to survive. I live with all that has shaped me, I love the shapes that I am, and I will continue to live, knowing what I have survived.

After my relationship with X finally ended, I thought that truly letting go of him meant forgetting about the pain and working my way back to a "pure place." I yearned to return to a place that predated the pain, back to a youthful naivete that would allow me to forget his name. I felt "dirty" as a survivor. Furthermore, because I had returned to him so many times, I stopped talking to anybody close to me about the relationship. I remember telling one friend that I had returned to him after the assault, and they responded in frustration by saying, "I don't want to hear about this anymore. You're asking for it at this point." Though I knew their frustrations came from a place of care, it made me feel like I deserved the pain that I was experiencing.

"Why didn't you leave?" Gayle King asked FKA twigs in an interview on *CBS This Morning*,* discussing twigs's experiences with her abusive relationship. Here is twigs's response:

> I think we just have to stop asking that question. I know that you're asking it, like, out of love, but like I'm just gonna make a stance and say that I'm not gonna answer that question anymore,

---

*Trigger Warning: The interview contains graphic descriptions of intimate violence and abuse. You can watch an excerpt from it, if you think you have the emotional capacity, on YouTube at youtube.com/watch?v=zR913A O2kMc.

because the question should really be to the abuser, "Why are you holding someone hostage with abuse?" People say, "Oh it can't have been that bad because or else she would have left." It's like, "No, it's because it was that bad, I couldn't leave."

Her powerful response struck me, and it dimmed the harsh spotlight that shame had cast on me. It allowed me to reframe the question from "What is wrong with me?" to "What is wrong in this relationship, and why do I feel like I cannot leave?" As I engaged in the tumultuous on-again, off-again toxic relationship, I sank deep into isolation, self-punishment, and shame. Very rarely did I consider the power dynamics involved, and the many ways I had been lied to, convinced, and coerced to stay. My shame unraveled into a cycle of self-destruction. I believed that my entire being was wrong, and therefore unworthy of love.

Our ending was abrupt, and I was completely devastated when he left. On top of that, I was ashamed of my devastation, convincing myself that I should be gleeful because I was free. I was still spiritually and emotionally tethered to the relationship. I was grieving, and furthermore, I was ashamed of that grief. I was mourning the familiar and consistent patterns of love-bombing, violence, and empty promises of accountability. When FKA twigs used the word "hostage" to describe her abuser's hold on her, I was reminded of the physical, emotional, and spiritual challenges it took to detach myself from X. I recalled times when he had threatened to call my close friends and tell them that I was still with him. His manipulation was frightening because he held me hostage to my own shame. He trapped me until I no longer knew what it meant to be free, and he knew that instilling shame in me was a tool he could use to control me. He no longer needed to physically force me to stay with him because I had learned how to manipulate myself into staying on my own.

I punished myself, insulted myself, and echoed the slander that he projected, and for a while I continued to self-destruct on my own. I was so ashamed of what felt like a painful addiction that I thrust myself deeper into it. I craved so deeply to un-meet him, for him to never have been in my life, and for his presence to cease to exist. When I realized that none of those things could happen, I had to focus on centering myself. I needed to unlearn shame to feel courageous enough to ask for help.

Unfortunately, survivors can be met with so much blame that it can be traumatic and painful to ask for help. There are resources for varying needs and requirements of survivors that we should be encouraged to access without shame. It was only after I sought guidance from specific organizations that I finally started to see the dissolution of our relationship as a blessing. What replaced the shame was a hope for healing and a determination to relearn new patterns of love. I had to accept that I could neither un-meet him nor undo the past, but I could navigate those hauntings with guidance and a renewed sense of compassion. As I allowed others to meet me with all my pain, I found the courage to meet myself again.

Just as we would do in grief, perhaps getting to know our ghosts will allow us to release them to embark on their safe voyages home. Even as our ghosts linger, they are there to remind us how potent and necessary our healing is. Some of us inherit ghosts from the moment we are born, and it takes a long time to get to know them with compassion. It is when we embrace ourselves fully, hauntings and all, that we can forgive ourselves enough to provide permission to heal. I had to ask myself many tender and difficult questions and get to know my hurt on a deep intimate level. I traced my pain back to childhood relationships and even my ancestry. I also had to see that X's actions reflected his own suffering, and that my top priority was to protect my spirit from his festering shame.

I will never return to a place pre-abuse, and as hard as I have tried, I will never forget X. My body, mind, and spirit will always have survived the brute force of his violence, and although none of that harm can be undone, my soma will also always remember how I slowly learned to untether, and how I had the courage to speak to loved ones about my experiences, reach out for therapy, receive the treatment of holistic medicine,* and support fellow survivors. I must continuously remind myself about the deepest lesson I learned as a survivor of intimate partner violence: I did not deserve the pain, but what I did in my survival was a testament to the love that endures in my spirit. It was messy, impure, and imperfect, and I did what I could with the tools that I had. I am devoted to relearning love without embodying shame.

What about the ghosts that linger when we have caused harm? After X, I chaotically ventured into many short-term relationships without taking my lovers seriously. I used people for company and

---

*My dear friends Fariha Róisín and Prinita Thevarajah compiled a list of QTPOC holistic medicine practitioners on their website Studio Ānanda. You can check it out at studioananda.space/practitioners.

validation when I was feeling heartbroken and low, and my actions hurt people's feelings. Afterward, I sat in shame with those actions and, for a long time, cut myself off from romance altogether. I punished myself even more, and I felt that any hope for my transformation was gone.

There is a difference between guilt and shame. In an article titled "Coping with Borderline Personality Disorder Embarrassment and Shame,"* Kristalyn Salters-Pedneault, PhD, differentiated the two by saying that guilt is the feeling you get when you are aware that you have *done* something wrong, while shame is the state of being that tells you that *your entire self* is wrong. What Dr. Salters-Pedneault is saying is that we are not inherently bad, even though our behavior can be. We are not the harmful action but the whole, complex (and usually traumatized) person who enacted it. It's not about absolving ourselves from responsibility but instead making a wider space to understand our full selves. When we can see ourselves, we can assess our harmful behavior, the roots of our pain, and what we can do to change.

In *The Politics of Trauma*, Staci K. Haines defines shame as "the generalized sense that we are wrong, bad, tainted, stupid, that it is *all* our fault. It is a deep and often hidden feeling that something is very wrong with us. Shame is the pervasive sense that we *are* wrong, not that we *did* something wrong." Shame triggers a spiral that leads us to detrimental self-punishment; instead of creating possibilities for change, shame makes us feel like everything is caving in on us. Guilt, on the other hand, is an uncomfortable awareness of our *actions*. It can drive us toward a recognition of our

---

*You can read the full article online at verywellmind.com/bpd-and-shame-425474.

responsibilities and what we must do to atone for our mistakes, especially if we have caused harm to others. Guilt can bring us closer to facing the consequences we need to face when we have enacted harm. It can help us create change, make amends, forge new patterns, invite openness, and do what we can to assist in healing the people we may have harmed (which can also mean giving space). It is important to listen to our guilt without becoming engulfed by it.

When shame festers, it can create even more harm. The more we sit in shame, the more expansive it becomes, not just to the self, but to everyone involved. A common phrase in the Western world in response to somebody causing harm is "You should be ashamed of yourself." However, just because somebody is ashamed of themselves does not mean they are equipped to stop acting in harmful ways. Sometimes it can be just the opposite: because they might believe that they are "bad" and condemned to a life of "wrongdoing," they are not inclined to heal or transform. While I believe that people who have enacted abuse should use their guilt as a generative force toward accountability, shame feels like a dead end.

As I was unlearning shame in my being, I had to reflect on the ways that shame pulsates through our culture. Instead of reducing harm, punishment and shame can prohibit us from practicing true accountability, and can even generate a sense of defensiveness. If we have been harmed, sinking into shame can prohibit us from accessing resources, reaching out for support and guidance, and believing in our healing. If we have caused harm, shame can create a hard protective shell around us that stops us from the difficult but necessary process it takes to reduce harm, atone for our mistakes, and make sure that we not repeat the harm that was enacted. Healing shame is vital in practicing accountability and making sure that harmful behaviors are not replicated. Shame shouts and puts a firm halt on transformative healing. It throws me deep into a grave of self-loathing, and who benefits from my self-hatred?

We need to learn how to engage in the difficult process of accountability, and the first step is listening to our guilt and learning how to apologize. While some apologies may not adequately repair severe forms of harm, apologies can be starting points to nurturing relationships and embarking on processes of accountable self-awareness. Mia Mingus, a writer and an educator who specializes in transformative justice and disability justice, elaborated on the nature of true and centered accountability in her two-part blog post* "The Four Parts of Accountability: How to Give a Genuine Apology Part 1" and "How to Give a Genuine Apology Part 2: The Apology—the What and the How." In the first blog post, she defines true accountability.

> True accountability, by its very nature, should push us to grow and change, to transform. Transformation is not to be romanticized or taken lightly. Remember, true transformation requires a death and a birth, an ending and a beginning. True accountability requires vulnerability and courage, two qualities that we are not readily encouraged to practice in our society.

Mingus's two-part guide on apologies is written specifically for "conflict, hurt, misunderstandings, small breaks in trust, and low-level harm," which she emphasizes is a pivotal starting point for accountability. We must be able to navigate the smaller conflicts to begin thinking about transformative consequences for larger and

---

*You can read the blog post in its entirety on Mia Mingus's blog at leaving evidence.wordpress.com.

more violent forms of harm. Her work is useful, clear, and concise, and provides readers with a thoughtful guide to starting their own interpersonal processes of accountability and being in right relationship with one another.

According to Mingus's guide, the four parts of a sincere apology are **self-reflection**, **apologizing**, **repair**, and **behavior change**. The first step, **self-reflection**, allows the perpetrator of harm to sit with their actions and contemplate on the harm caused. This requires immense self-awareness and a dedication to repairing a sacred relationship. The second step, **apologizing**, must include the specific words "I am sorry" and the naming of both the harm that was caused and the impact of said harm. The third step, **repair**, is "a uniquely challenging part of accountability because it must be done in relationship and cannot be done alone, unlike changing one's behavior"; therefore, it takes a *consensual* rebuilding of trust and requires much vulnerability. The fourth step, **behavior change**, takes a commitment to changing our actions and not enacting the harm again. According to Mingus, "This step is key because it doesn't matter how great your apology was if you continue the hurt or harm."

My favorite section of Mia Mingus's blog post emphasizes how we should treat apologizing as a sacred act:

Apologizing is part of accountability and accountability is a sacred practice of love. If you've hurt someone you care about, it is sacred work to tend to that hurt. You are caring for this person, the relationship you share, as well as yourself. You are engaging in the sacred work of accountability, healing, and being in right relationship. This work is part of the broader legacy of transformative justice, love, and interdependence.

Included in her two-part guide are tips to execute the sincerest apologies possible. They include addressing harm as soon as possible, being fully present for the apology, being proactive, building a culture of accountability, letting go of outcome and control, and practicing toward the sincerest apologies possible. She stresses that "apologizing to someone so that they will apologize to you is not apologizing—it is manipulation." While you cannot control the outcome of the apology, becoming dedicated to accountability means committing to finding resources that will help you not replicate the harm that you caused. Apologies are key in the continuance of caring and loving relationships. They are an opportunity to rebuild trust and repair and deepen relationships, not only with one another, but also with ourselves.

X's constant apologies were usually insincere because he did not take action to atone for his violence. His apologies were still tools of manipulation, and he was only expressing them to control the desired outcome of our reunion. While he may have had an initial awareness, he did not move beyond the second step of the accountability process. He did not engage in repairing or changing his behaviors, and just saying the words "I'm sorry" did not constitute an accountable apology. X's severe harm required a lot more than an apology, although if we widen our view, we will see that we do not live in a culture that encourages accountability or atonement for severe harm. Instead, we are offered options that are entwined with carceral punishment. Building on Mingus's four parts of accountability, how do we ensure accountability when it comes to severe forms of harm? And how do we make sure that our efforts are always centered on survivors?

Perhaps while reading my personal retellings of abuse, you wondered why I never involved the police. After both the alleyway assault and the rape, I did consider calling the police because I was not sure what else to do. Most people I reached out to told me to do the same. However, I was undocumented at the time and did not feel safe involving the state at any capacity. I also did not know what measures they would take with X, though I knew that their methods would not encourage him to change. I knew that with prosecution came intense punishment, and although the fantasy of his suffering temporarily satiated me, I knew that there would not be true justice. Calling the police to arrest X would not stop his violence. Furthermore, I was paranoid that doing so would lead him to become vengeful toward me. It spoke volumes that I did not feel safe, protected, or secure in relation to either X or the carceral state.

The ethic of punishment has been seeded in most of us since birth and it surrounds us everywhere we go. If we look at carceral systems, especially in the United States, we will see that prisons are places designed to target people, especially Black people in America, and force them into violent, racist, traumatizing spaces of isolation and punishment. The US carceral system was built on anti-Black racism and violence, and police forces originated during times of chattel slavery. The movement for abolition was created by Black feminist civil rights activists to put an end to enslavement.

Unfortunately, despite these revolutionary movements, the police state has continued to evolve, and abolitionists continue to strategize, organize, and fight for the end of the prison industrial complex and police brutality. In *We Do This 'Til We Free Us*,* abolitionist Mariame Kaba writes that the carceral system is not broken—in fact, it is *operating exactly as it was intended to*.† The carceral state's intentions were always rooted in shame, punishment, torture, and white supremacy.

Carceral systems actively attempt to distract us from their harm by masquerading as the perpetrators of justice. They deliberately tap into imaginary binaries of good versus evil and mass-manipulate people into believing that only some are worthy of abundance and resources, while others are disposable and punishable. The carceral system does not honor life, relationships, or transformation, and it does not care about healing or justice. Degrading conditions in prisons and solitary confinement deliberately try to strip people of community. Prison operators and police have never cared for justice or the well-being and safety of Black, brown, disabled, immigrant, and working-class people.

We must think long-term when we think about consequences. Abolitionists such as Ida B. Wells, Ruth Wilson Gilmore, Mariame Kaba, K Agbebiyi, Dr. Angela Y. Davis, Tamara K. Nopper, and Jackie Wang, to name a few, write extensively on prison abolition and explore a range of alternatives and possibilities.‡ They do not

---

*I will be using this seminal book as a guide for those learning about abolition throughout this chapter—I highly recommend that you read it!

†This is from her essay "The System Isn't Broken" in *We Do This 'Til We Free Us*.

‡There are abolitionist writings included in the Recommendations for Further Reading at the end of this book.

deny that there needs to be consequences when it comes to harm, but they are firm in arguing that prisons and the carceral state do not offer transformation and justice. Even when the person in question may have caused immense violence and harm, it is crucial to ask whether locking them up in a jail cell will truly allow for long-term transformation. We also cannot neglect investigating the systemic violence that may have caused people to commit harm in the first place. Instead of funding the police, we need to fund health care, education, housing, and therapy. The carceral system is a tattered Band-Aid that infects wounds with no interest in healing them.

In *I Hope We Choose Love*, Kai Cheng Thom writes, "Trauma dictates that justice must be punitive for us to feel safe. Paradoxically, of course, punitive justice tends to diminish our safety because it involves hurting other people and makes them far less likely to be accountable of their own volition." I had to unpack this paradox and ask myself some difficult questions: Would X's imprisonment really end the violence against me or his future partners? Would his shameful isolation encourage him to do accountability work and healing? Would the police protect me? Do I feel safe around the police, or anybody who works in law enforcement? What other options do I have, and who can support and protect me? I had to ask these difficult questions to consider my safety as a survivor while also advocating for transformative justice.

Many domestic violence survivors do not feel safe calling the police. Police and prison guards are enactors of the very same strains of harassment, violence, and sexual assault. While I often wanted to see X suffer for the harm he had caused, I also knew that sending him to prison would not transform him, and perhaps even make him more violent and rageful. Mariame Kaba goes into detail about this in her essay "Yes, We Mean Literally Abolish the Police," which appears in *We Do This 'Til We Free Us.**

Two-thirds of people who experience sexual violence never report it to anyone. Those who file police reports are often dissatisfied with the response. Additionally, police officers themselves commit sexual assault alarmingly often. A study in 2010 found that sexual misconduct was the second most frequently reported form of police misconduct. In 2015, the *Buffalo News* found that an officer was caught for sexual misconduct every five days.

In an interview with Ayana Young in her podcast, *For the Wild,*[†] Mariame Kaba said,

The fact of the matter is that more than 50 percent of people who are harmed, very badly harmed by the way, never contact law enforcement at all in the first place. And so that means they prefer nothing at all, as my friend Danielle Sered says, from Common Justice. They prefer nothing at all rather than what we currently offer.

Furthermore, Kaba wrote in *We Do This 'Til We Free Us*: "So You're Thinking about Becoming an Abolitionist,"[‡]

---

*This essay was originally published in *The New York Times* in June 2020.

†You can listen to and read a transcript of the episode "Mariame Kaba on Moving Past Punishment /151" on *For the Wild*'s website: forthewild.world/listen/mariame-kaba-on-moving-past-punishment-151.

‡This essay first appeared in *LEVEL* in October 2020.

If we want to reduce (or end) sexual and gendered violence, putting a few perpetrators in prison does little to stop the many other perpetrators. It does nothing to change a culture that makes this harm imaginable, to hold the individual perpetrator accountable, to support their transformation, or to meet the needs of the survivors.

Being an abolitionist does not mean that you do not believe in consequences for the actions of abusers, especially if they have caused severe harm. The core precedent of abolition is to always center and prioritize the survivor's safety. Abolition calls for *true* transformative consequences while dismantling state-sanctioned forms of punishment. All harm cannot be lumped together, and there are many varying levels of harm that require varying levels of consequence. Once again, Kaba explains it to us clearly, this time in her essay with Rachel Herzing in *We Do This 'Til We Free Us*: "Transforming Punishment: What Is Accountability without Punishment?," which primarily explores abolition in relation to R. Kelly's violent actions.

> While abolitionists hold a range of values, principles, and ideas about transformation, we've never known an abolitionist who thought that nothing was the preferred alternative to imprisonment. We believe in consequences for harm, for Kelly or anyone else.
>
> Those consequences may involve forgoing royalties and any future financial gain derived from the context in which the harm occurred, or being required to pay restitution or provide labor to those who have been harmed, their families, and when appropriate, their communities.

Those consequences might include restricted access to specific groups or spaces, or ineligibility for positions of leadership. Consequences might also include being required to make a public apology. Regardless of what's chosen, the point is that any consequences should be determined in direct relationship to the harm done and should involve input by people impacted by the harm.

Upon reading this essay, I felt the fog of my personal confusion begin to clear. It gave me newfound agency to consider the consequences I thought would be suitable for X's actions toward me, and it felt liberating to think that a survivor could have input on those consequences. In retrospect, the first consequence that would have been helpful after the assault was making certain that X stayed far away from me by ensuring that I had a support system in place to make this happen. To a certain extent, that did happen after the assault. With the help of some dear friends in the community, I told a few nightlife organizers, who proceeded to ban X from the events I frequented. Furthermore, I needed a support system that could deny him access to my address and personal information because it was so difficult for me to do so on my own. I needed resources to help me unlearn my own shame, stop returning to him, and stay grounded in my healing. I needed *his* support system (his friends and family) to make sure that he took some space from alcohol and dating and went through intensive therapy.

It might be overwhelming to think of alternatives to the violent carceral system, but we must support one another in thinking of alternatives in the effort. Yeshimabeit "Yeshi" Milner, the director of Data for Black Lives, wrote that the practice of abolition is an act of creation.* While we endeavor to destroy violent systems, we are also actively planting nourishing seeds for new forms of justice and care. It is completely possible to dismantle and destroy the violent systems of colonization, slavery, and imprisonment; abolitionists have been turning those dreams into reality for a very long time.

We can replace (not reform) these carceral systems with alternatives that emphasize care, consequences, accountability, justice, and healing. Many people feel resistant to abolition because they think that the concept is too radical. However, abolitionists have done the work and drafted extremely precise, intentional, and detailed alternatives to the carceral system. An online resource called #8toabolition[†] offers a guide to an abolitionist future. The website details eight demands: **defund police, demilitarize communities, remove police from schools, free people from jails and prisons, repeal laws that criminalize survival, invest in community self-governance, provide safe housing for everyone,** and **invest in care, not cops.** The guide is incredibly expansive and clear and is a testament to the groundbreaking work that abolitionists are committed to.

In an emergency, we often think that the police are the only people we can call. Our resources already feel limited, and the police have a strong presence in our everyday lives. Abolitionists have worked on hotlines and alternative resources for people

---

*You can read her work and watch her speak at her blog: medium.com /@yeshican.

†#8toabolition was created by Mon Mohapatra, Leila Raven, Nnennaya Amuchie, Reina Sultan, K Agbebiyi, Sarah T. Hamid, Micah Herskind, Derecka Purnell, Eli Dru, and Rachel Kuo. You can find it at 8toabolition .com.

seeking immediate help. The online directory Don't Call the Police* provides alternatives in every state in the United States, as well as some provinces in Canada. There are safe houses and shelters that provide safe spaces for survivors. For example, Freedom House is a domestic violence shelter for people with disabilities that also welcomes people without disabilities. The Anti Police-Terror Project in Oakland and the Community Action Teams 911 (CAT-911) in Los Angeles are two other alternatives. Many twenty-four-hour hotlines that provide emergency support in different languages are also listed on Don't Call the Police.

Carceral systems of punishment have taken up residence in the hearts, spirits, and minds of so many of us. Our interrogation of the violence of the carceral state will reveal that many of its poisons have seeped into our psyches. The carceral state knowingly capitalizes on our feelings of shame, isolation, and disposability to continue its violent history of brutality. It plants its poisonous seeds inside us so that we move toward an ethic of punishment because we do not know justice without it. We need to imagine what it is like to move away from punishment and toward long-term consequences and healing centered on survivors. Following the wisdom of the Black anarchist Greg Jackson to "kill the cop in your head," we must remember to abolish the police that live in our hearts, the ones who whisper blame and shame in our ears, who instill anti-Blackness in us all, and who block us from true centered accountability and healing. We must be committed to abolishing the police if we also wish to end sexual assault, intimate partner violence, and systemic racism.

---

*Go to dontcallthepolice.com to see a list of alternatives to calling the cops. Additional resources are at the back of this book.

When somebody is acting abusively, naming them as an abuser clarifies that harm has been caused. It helps to identify the specific relational and power dynamics involved. But when we look at the abuser's other relationships spanning from childhood to adulthood, it's possible they may be survivors too. Both realities can coexist. As a survivor of intimate partner violence who is committed to and still learning about abolition, I have become familiar with the complexities of coexisting realities.

As a survivor, I have learned about the profundities of both/and. The stark binaries of good/evil, peaceful/violent, innocent/guilty, and even survivor/abuser often tend to fail us. Most of the time, abusers have experienced abuse themselves, and their harmful behaviors tend to be replicas of harm they witnessed or experienced since childhood. None of this makes the abuser's behavior acceptable, but it points to a larger problem that is usually swept under oversimplifications of good versus bad. When we critically think about why trauma happens and how it travels from one generation to the next, a messy spiral of intergenerational and state-sanctioned trauma unfurls. It pushes us to ask why violence happens in the first place and who is responsible for our suffering. Our love is interconnected, and our hurt is interconnected too.

I knew that X had experienced and witnessed abuse in his childhood, and in many ways, his brutality toward me mirrored the abuse that he'd seen in his family. His earliest ideas of love were informed by patriarchal violence, and therefore his reenactments of "love" demonstrated the same thing. He was haunted by ghosts. While this does not excuse his abusive behavior, it showed me that the environments he grew up in were not disconnected from the systemic racism and violence that his family had experienced as immigrants in the United States. People cause harm because they have a relationship with harm themselves. By acknowledging that everybody has been in relationship with harm, the bigger question is how we can put an end to systemic violence and prevent these reenactments of harm. From the framework of transformative justice, we need to simultaneously hold all these truths to make sure that we heal from all forms of violence, both systemic and interpersonal.

When I saw X break down after he first assaulted me, I knew that he held a lot of shame in his heart. The shame had bubbled and blistered, and eventually it spilled out of him as violence. He had forced himself into a suffocating box, and he continued to hurt me because he did not know how to break the toxic patterns. When he apologized, he often used self-deprecating language that held no promise of change. When he broke down in front of me, he would always say that there was something wrong with him, that he was beyond saving, and that he was a bad person who needed my love. He could have used his guilt as a generative source of energy to identify his violent actions and seek the help that he needed. Instead, he festered in his shame, and still never explored the ways that he could heal or actively treat me better. He did not learn from his violence and even victimized himself within it. He passed his hauntings on to me.

It is difficult to exercise accountability if it is not normalized as a constant committed practice. It is also very challenging to be accountable when we feel isolated in our shame. Accountability is a community process and requires ongoing conversations, check-ins, imaginings, and resources that will allow a perpetrator of harm to acknowledge that they have committed harm. The people who chose to stay friends with X, even after knowing about his abusive behavior, assumed the responsibility of holding him accountable. Instead, they abdicated that responsibility and avoided the conversation altogether. As his proclaimed community, they should have engaged in difficult conversations that encouraged X to take a break from romantic relationships, cease alcohol consumption, and receive intensive mental health care.

It is not my responsibility to show compassion toward X, even though, in my most vulnerable hours, I have. I do not apologize for any abuser's behaviors, and I no longer dedicate time or energy toward helping X heal. I hope that he channels his guilt into enactments of ongoing healing, because that is the only way he can put an end to his violent patterns. As for myself, I am no longer interested in self-punishment, for it takes away from the compassion that is needed for me to focus on my healing. I honor my own survival to the highest degree, and I want to make sure that I do not replicate violence that I have experienced. I am devoted to putting an end to intimate partner violence and sexual assault, which means that I must also be dedicated to transformative justice that does not operate solely on shame and punishment. All of these realities coexist.

When we can discern that our actions, instead of our inherent beings, are harmful, we can also focus on those actions and learn how to do better. We can ask ourselves crucial questions that explore the origins of our harm and trauma and seek the help we need from there. Instead of sinking into a self-punishing despair, we can show ourselves compassion by being committed to atoning

for our actions and making sure that we never replicate our harmful actions. Shame fogs our clarity and almost becomes an obsession with self-deprecation. To break our harmful patterns, we must
be willing to clearly see those patterns first. We can transfer our
guilty energy into a determination for accountability.

Mia Mingus writes about this in a blog post titled "Dreaming
Accountability":*

> We can start with our self-accountability and the ways that we
> don't show up for *ourselves*. We can acknowledge how most of us
> are in an abusive relationship with ourselves. We blow past our
> own boundaries, we punish and beat ourselves up in terrible
> ways. We can start with the ways we treat and talk to ourselves—
> ways that we would clearly recognize as abuse if it were being
> done to another person.

As we live with our ghosts, we must get to know them better.
Shame forces us to push them away as they howl at us. But running
from our hauntings only intensifies their presence. Like all the
emotions I talk about, the ghosts of our guilt are trying to communicate something very vital to us. They provide us with a window
into seeing what we wish to transform, how we wish to unlearn,
and how to hold ourselves deeply accountable. Listening to our
ghosts, instead of running away from them, allows us to break
generational curses. I share with you these profound questions
that Mia Mingus asks:

---

*You can read this wonderful blog post at leavingevidence.wordpress.com
/2019/05/05/dreaming-accountability-dreaming-a-returning-to-ourselves-and
-each-other/.

What if we rushed towards our own accountability and understood it as a gift we can give to ourselves and those hurting from our harm? What if we understood our accountability, not as some small insignificant act, but as an intentional drop in an ever-growing river of healing, care, and repair that had the potential to nourish, comfort and build back trust on a large scale, carving new paths of hope and faith through mountains of fear and unacknowledged pain for generations?

My self-hatred and shame do not benefit anybody—not myself, my relationships, my healing, or my dreams. If I am honest about the mistakes that I have made while healing from the harm I have endured, I am being wholly loving to myself and all the people I deeply care about. When my shame melts away, I can ask for the help and support I deserve. What guilt illuminates to me is the importance of relationships, and how difficult and challenging it can be to be in right relationship with one another, including myself. I strive to listen to the ghosts of my guilt without drowning in shame, which means that I must learn to live with them and no longer resist myself.

My ghosts still float around me, though I have allowed myself to get to know them better. Some of them have drifted away, to the spirit world, though some of them still linger. This does not mean that I live in the past, but that I allow them to hover with me in the present. While at first it was difficult to look them in the eye, I know that avoiding them pushed me further from my loving truth. I am not broken, even though my heart has been. I am not beyond repair, because I am constantly regenerating. I do not wish to cause harm, though sometimes I may do so unintentionally. If I do cause harm, my ghosts generously remind me of the importance of my relationships, and I am encouraged to be courageous in my accountability. My ghosts tell me that I cannot travel back in time or undo the damage that has been done, and that my commitment to being loving needs to be rooted in the now.

I cannot return to my former self, as I exist in the multidimensions of the present. Here, I am met with a plethora of realities and a plethora of selves. The conditions of punishment have long been planted inside me, and the only way I can unlearn the sharpness of shame is by engaging deeply with my active imagination. With the help of abolitionists, organizers, educators, friends, family, and lovers, we can collectively dream into being what true accountability, sincere apologies, transformative justice, and healthy, loving relationships can be. While I know that the world cannot return to a place of pre-abuse, I can imagine a world that transforms and thrives beyond these forms of violence. I can see us shedding our shame and attentively listening to our guilt. I can imagine us breaking patterns of intergenerational pain. As the world regenerates, so do we. In fact, I do not just have to imagine it, for I feel it, close to my heart.

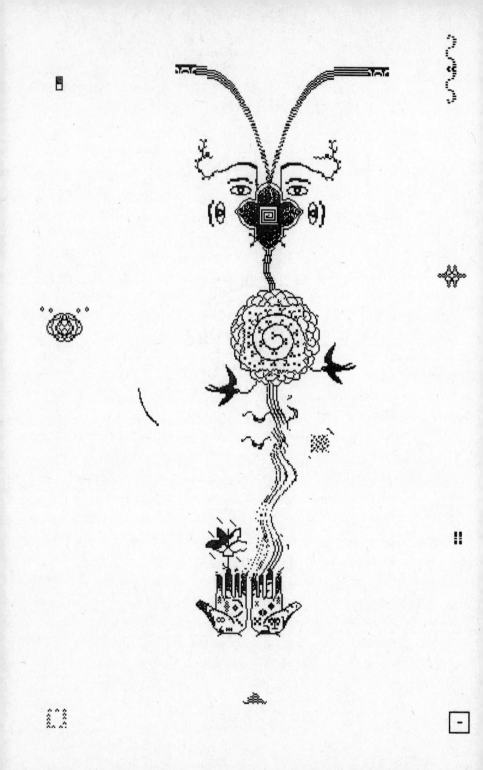

SEVEN

PRESENCE

Meeting My Multitudes Again

I fell in love one hot day at an estuary in Puerto Rico.* An estuary is the meeting place between two bodies of water, a family reunion where river runs into sea. Time moved differently on that tropical day; it moved by birdsong, cloud formations, the drop of ripe passion fruit, and the bloom of a hibiscus flower. As I waded into the cold river, I was reminded of my childhood. I had grown up mostly in tropical climates, and as I traversed farther into the estuary, I met the familiarity of the warm ocean. A memory came to mind: I was at a Singaporean beach as a moody teenager, and I was playfully sucking on the nectar of an ixora flower while wallowing in the ocean. I plucked an ixora

---

*Thank you, Gabe, for bringing me to this sacred place.

flower from a tree in Puerto Rico and did the same. As I sat in the intersection between the warm salty ocean and the chilly clear fresh water, I felt my childhood and adult selves merge. More accurately, I realized that they were never apart, and that they were connected by all threads of life. I met myself again this way, and I fell in love.

The estuary is the perfect union and a miraculous meeting place. Fresh water and salt water flow into each other and it feels like a homecoming. Estuaries are home to all sorts of beings: moss, tadpoles, fish, and seaweed. As I waded in during sunset, it felt like a reunion, familiar and new and exciting all the same. It was both warm and cold, depending on where I chose to be. I sat with her, immersed in her textures, layers, temperatures, and life. I thought about how the ocean is usually seen as the life force that separates all the continents, and very quickly realized that was not the case. The ocean does not divide the land; she is a sacred connector, and she connects us all. That day, she gifted me the opportunity to reconnect my own dots and learn of my multiple dimensions. All I had to do was sit with her.

I could feel the soft breath of the ocean intertwine with the stillness of the river. I sat in the middle of this abundant diverse environment and reflected on the times in my life where meetings of synchronicity felt as destined as this meeting between river and sea. In the estuary, I met my childhood self, my heartbroken self, my healing self, my toxic self, my joyous self, my insecure self, my curious self, my fearful self, and my loving self. I met myself as lover, friend, sibling, and child. All my dimensions coalesced with the water, the sun, the sand, and the humid air. In interconnected presence, we all merged into one.

When lovers meet, not only do they come together to build on mutual attraction and common interests, but they also get to know each other's differences too. I have spent so much time romanticizing meeting lovers; sitting in stillness with the estuary gave me a sacred moment to contemplate what it means to meet myself as lover and friend. My relationship with myself was one that I had neglected for so long. In that deep moment of presence, I rekindled many dimensions, and I was able to see my own contradictions and fluidities come together as fertile, flowing, and abundant. Not only did I meet myself, but I also met everything that I am inseparable from. Nothing is separate, everything is interconnected, and we are all here, now.

To meet myself again, I must be open to presence. Presence is not just a practice; it is a state of embodied being. In moments of presence, there is a merging of many dimensions. I am in touch with my body, heart, spirit, and mind, not only as an individual being but as someone who is interconnected with all beings in the universe. I am in touch with every waking moment, each sacred breath, each pebble, leaf, and breeze that reminds me of my aliveness. Words do not adequately describe the euphoria of true embodied presence; it must be felt, and requires time, patience, and release. Presence seems simple because it exists at the core of our everyday existence. So why does embodying presence feel so hard?

Stillness has become a privilege for many. While one might not always require stillness to achieve a sense of presence, experiencing stillness is one of the fundamental and forgotten ways to remind us to pay attention to our breath and beingness. Practices such as meditation and deep intentional breathing allow an opening for mind, body, and spirit. So many people feel that they cannot afford to be still, or they feel guilty when permitting themselves moments of stillness, and some people literally cannot afford to allocate long periods of time to stillness because we live in a society that requires generational wealth or constant work to afford necessities. Stillness is deliberately made inaccessible and out of reach. Our phones teach us to navigate life at a quickened pace, one that disconnects us from the patience of Earth. We are surrounded by subliminal messages that urge us to move quickly, to consume, and to embrace distraction. When our survival depends on us running to keep up with the fast pace of late-stage capitalism, slowing down feels like either a luxury or a forgotten thing of the past.

Bayo Akomolafe is a writer and scholar who teaches about "slowing down in urgent times." In a conversation with Ayana Young on the podcast *For the Wild*,* he said,

I literally had a German brother write to me and say that "Your slowing down invocation isn't working because my bosses are still on my neck. Slowing down to type a memo isn't really working," and I responded by saying, "Slowing down is not a function

---

*You can listen to, and read a transcript of, the episode "Bayo Akomolafe on Slowing Down in Urgent Times /155" at forthewild.world/listen/bayo-akomolafe-on-slowing-down-in-urgent-times-155.

of speed, [it] is a function of awareness, and I don't want to make awareness a mental construct. It's a function of presence." So, when I invite slowing down, I invite us to research, to perform research into the ancestral tentacularities that proceed from us. I'm asking us to touch our bodies and touch our colonial bubbles. I'm asking us to listen, as you say, to witness, no not just to witness, to "with-ness"; to be with land, and community, and ancestor, and progeny, and children in a way that isn't instrumental.

Although the English language often fails me, the best way I can describe embodied presence is reminiscent to the visceral sensations of falling in love. When you meet somebody special and engage in an intimate relationship with them, you become hyperaware of their habits and actions that nobody else gets to see. As you fall in love with them, you see who they are beyond their public performance, how they engage with the world, what excites and saddens them, and you cherish every breath they take. I have felt so deeply present in the company of lovers, including X, because there were so many shared memories of when we were both wholly engaged and present. They still feel so crisp, alive, and new, and are impossible to forget. I remember every interconnected sensation and detail from these moments: delicate sunbeams, the crash of the ocean, an eyelash falling on his face. During these moments, the only thing that mattered was that everything was in interbeing and aliveness. I felt alive and in love with our shared life. Yet falling in love with another person is not the only time we experience embodied presence. While we are encouraged to seek romance and partnerships, I must wonder, when are we encouraged to feel this way with ourselves?

On Earth, there are many ways to measure time. Streams of water move and trickle at their own velocity, trees grow at their own pace, towering rocks shape-shift over centuries, and insects live lifetimes that seem small to us but are full to them. Most of these time frames seem to revolve around the continuance of everyday survival. Perhaps nonhuman beings do not count time in days, but live each passing moment through warmth, light, sunrise, and sunset. Modern human civilization, however, measures time in days, hours, and minutes that revolve around work and productivity.* When our time is measured by work, subconsciously, so is our worth. When we stop working, we may not know what to do with ourselves. We may find work so strenuous and exhausting that we spend the rest of our time distracting ourselves. We could find ourselves only semi-present in everything we do and therefore absent or dissociative at work, rest, and play.

In *Severance*, Ling Ma's novel released in 2018, a pandemic called the Shen Fever took over the world. The disease was spread by a fungal spore that originated in Shenzhen, China. The story was set in New York City, and was told from the perspective of Candace Chen, an introspective Chinese American woman who was a disgruntled employee at a book publishing company. As people became rapidly infected, they would engage in cycles of behavior

---

*An amazing book about the attention economy that you can read is Jenny Odell's *How to Do Nothing*.

that would lead to their deaths. They would get caught in trances that they could not get out of, and they would usually do mundane and common activities until they physically could not do them anymore, like trying on outfits, driving cars, and watching television. They were zombified by familiar and boring tasks. They would not drink water or eat food, and they would eventually die of starvation. As I read the book, I found that the most chilling case was set in an empty Times Square. Candace was walking through the eerily abandoned tourist destination and peered into the window of a Victoria's Secret. In the store there was an infected employee whose eyes were empty and whose repetitive actions were lifeless. She was folding clothes, repeatedly, even though every garment in the store was already tidily placed. Those were her final actions, and she died atop a pile of lingerie.

I read *Severance* before the COVID-19 pandemic began in 2020. Ling Ma's take on a zombie apocalypse was terrifying because it sounded familiar. She included specific brand names that were recognizable to me, and placed the reader in a city that has been heralded as the heart of business and capitalism. Imagining my own final actions was jarring, and I wondered what my final loop would be. Would I be looking in the mirror? Working at a mundane job? Scrolling mindlessly on my phone? The book forced me to contemplate what capitalism has pushed us to be devoted to. While we dedicate ourselves to hours, days, weeks, years of work to survive, what are we being forced to forget? What hypnotic states are we currently in? Why does it seem impossible to spend time like the river, the ocean, and the rocks?

Although COVID-19 is not identical to Shen Fever, there are many frightening parallels. Like Shen Fever, COVID-19 has exposed many gaping holes in capitalism. Systems of capitalism are built on greed, violence, and neglect, and actively attempt to steer us away from reflection and stillness. During the pandemic, when I was forced to sit in unfamiliar moments of silence, I found myself re-asking these questions with urgency: What am I devoting my time to? Who is controlling our fate? What have I forgotten? What is not working?

At the beginning of the pandemic, so many of us were forced to learn what to do with new measures of time. I lost my job and housing, was uncertain about my immigration status, and could no longer spend time with my friends or see my family. I could also no longer engage in the same toxic habits that I had turned into a lifestyle. All my usual distractions (socializing and partying) were gone. Suddenly I had a vast well of time to just be, which felt unfamiliar and scary. In that time, I was either desperately seeking distraction or sinking into a deep depression. When thoughts of X returned and unprocessed traumas resurfaced, I realized how much I needed guidance and support. How could I feel safe in my own presence? How could I seek guidance when we all had to be so far apart? No matter how hard I tried, I could not get away from myself. While we are taught to be individualistic and hyperproductive, we are not taught how to slowly tend to our relationships with ourselves. I had to meet myself again.

In a world that encourages constant movement at a speedy pace, there is so much we fail to notice. The pandemic revealed my fear of stillness, which was rooted in being frightened of what would be uncovered if I slowed down. When I was forced to finally slow down, I had to face so much unprocessed grief and many of my toxic addictions. I saw how I attached my worth to work and external validation. My intuition had always known that the shadows were lurking, which was why I had been urgently running away. Stillness allowed me to befriend my shadows, sit with them in solitude, and unlock a sense of presence. I noticed the pain that lingered and the heartbreak I harbored. And for the first time in a while, all this newfound time allowed me to notice my childlike curiosities, my quirks, my hobbies, my small pleasures, and my profound joy. Stillness opens an awareness of our aliveness. Presence allows us to remember who we are.

To come to full and embodied presence, we must learn how to let go. We need to release illusions of control, anxieties that gnaw at our minds, the heavy imprints of our egos, and the static energy of our fear. When I have been told to "let go," it always felt like an incomplete message to receive. Though it sounded simple, it always felt like a challenging and abstract practice. I wished for a list of instructions, calls to action, and tasks that could help me perform release. Everything I gathered felt inconclusive, and I still woke up from every slumber carrying a heavy weight on my chest. But the art of letting go does not always come with a list of actions. In fact, most of the time, it is succumbing to inaction, and accepting that no matter how hard we try, sometimes there is nothing more we can do except be. When I finally accepted that, I was ready to let go.

A year before the alleyway assault, X and I spent a summer weekend in Cairns, Queensland, at the Great Barrier Reef. He had just met my family and was experiencing the places I had explored as a child. Even as we spent time together in my childhood home, we got into miserable arguments that were becoming increasingly aggressive. At the same time, we shared some of the most intimate experiences that I have ever shared with a partner.

A big part of our relationship was venturing into psychedelic experiences together. Psychedelic plant medicine, such as magic mushrooms, helped us reconnect with our inner children and allowed our spirits to meet. Despite our frequent conflicts, anytime we took mushrooms together, it felt sacred and safe. Our inhibitions and insecurities faded away, and we were able to be present, curious, and in love. Sometimes it almost felt like we purposefully took psychedelic plant medicine to return to that place together. In Cairns, we took some mushrooms and explored the paradise of the tropics, were wooed by the mangroves, and amazed at the huge blue monarch butterflies that were migrating from one lush rain forest to another. We roamed the rain forest, hugged the trees, and watched a group of tourists gasp at the botanical wonders surrounding them. I felt safest with X when we went on those psychedelic trips.

I was walking where the ocean meets the sand, while he was playfully skidding through the puddles left by a tropical rainstorm. We were in our own worlds and still intricately interconnected. The sun had begun to set. It was a cacophony of pinks and purples and oranges, and as the sky dissolved in all her warm colors, I found myself mesmerized. I noticed the fluid shades and movements of every transforming cloud, and I saw once again the blue monarch butterflies fluttering by us right before nightfall. They were migrating, moving on with the breeze. The butterflies were passing us by, and I thought about taking photos and capturing the moment, or even trying to cup one in my hand, but I paused. Why did I feel so compelled to capture this moment, to freeze and preserve this beauty in time? These butterflies had to go where they were going, and I shook off the impulse to interrupt their safe passage home.

I looked at X in his own world. I thought of our relationship and knew that it had to pass through like the butterflies. The beauty of our relationship flashed before my eyes, as vibrant and romantic as the monarch's bright blue wings. I had wanted so many times to capture our relationship, put it in a jar, and preserve the good times before they turned sour. I held on to our relationship because I was determined to relive our beauty and replay it on a loop. As the butterflies became tiny specks on the horizon, I realized that I could no longer hold on to this terrifying and beautiful relationship. Trapping the butterfly would not have honored her impermanence. I could no longer force the beauty of intimacy. I looked deep into the hypnotic waves of the ocean as she, too, said good night to the sun. X looked at me and was surprised to see tears streaming down my face. I had no control over the demise of our relationship, and I knew that it had to end.

There are three sacred parts of enlightenment: **non-self**, **impermanence**, and **interbeing**. **Non-self** does not mean that we cease to exist, but that we do not exist as isolated beings. Our individualistic self does not exist because it is intertwined with everything, and therefore it is not a single entity but part of a greater "One." **Impermanence** is the acknowledgment that all things pass; it allows us to look toward grand perspectives beyond immediate feelings of pain. By accepting impermanence we free ourselves from the heavy binaries of life and death and save ourselves from constantly fearing impending doom. Doom passes too. All things regenerate. **Interbeing** is the acknowledgment that all things are interconnected; therefore, because I exist and am connected to everything, I will not fully cease to exist when I die. To achieve enlightenment, we must always be with these three sacred parts and release the desire to conquer our pain.

In *Letting Go*, David R. Hawkins defines letting go by using a Buddhist framework in his wisdoms.

> Letting go involves being aware of a feeling, letting it come up, staying with it, and letting it run its course without wanting to make it different or do anything about it. It means simply to let the feeling be there and to focus on letting out the energy behind it. The first step is to allow yourself to have the feeling without resisting it, venting it, fearing it, condemning it, or moralizing about it. It means to drop judgment and to see that it is *just* a feeling. The technique is to be with the feeling and surrender all efforts to modify it in any way. Let go of wanting to resist the feeling. *It is resistance that keeps the feeling going.*

Letting go is surrendering to the purity of being and the vivaciousness of presence. It is realizing that nothing matters and everything matters at the same time, because nothing and everything are connected. If I could offer any advice, the best thing to do when releasing ego-driven attachments is to go to wide open spaces where you can be surrounded by beings who also practice the art of enlightened presence. Go to the ocean, the forest, the desert, and see how each lapping wave, cluster of moss, and rock formation is actively letting go. Not only are they letting go of themselves in every second that they live, but they are also welcoming each new moment with full embodiment. They know that they, too, will pass.

For a long time, I did not know how to meditate. I held the misconception that meditation was completely clearing the mind and holding no thoughts. I tried to visualize blankness and nothingness, but found that while I was trying so hard not to think, my body was unable to relax. Exasperated, I stopped trying because it seemed too difficult. I later learned from Vietnamese Buddhist monks that meditation is not meant to force you into a state of non-thought. Meditation is about being immersed and relaxed with everything that exists in the now, even the pain, the joy, the confusion, and the fear. It is an orchestral congealing of every interconnected part of reality.

One winter's day, I traveled to upstate New York with my dear friend LoAn Nguyen* to visit a Vietnamese Buddhist monastery. After meditating for a few hours with a group of Vietnamese monks, we were taken on a walk around the monastery. There was

---

*Shout-out to my beloved friend and mentor LoAn, who teaches me every day about embodied love and presence. She also teaches me that presence can lead us to becoming clear about the causes we care for.

a forest that wrapped around the temple, and the monks encouraged us to explore in silence, calling this activity mindfulness walking. We were encouraged to take off our shoes and walk around freely, and the only instruction we were given was to breathe deep and feel the ground with each intentional step. As my toes touched the cold blades of grass, I felt the freezing damp moisture of the earth under my skin. I thought about the ways that we squirm at the touch of soil, how we have been taught to distrust the ground we walk on, and how concrete actively separates us from connecting directly to sacred land. We walked past outstretching branches, clusters of melting snow, and a frozen heart-shaped lake. This thirty-minute walk was transformative, and after a while I had forgotten about the cold and was relishing the magnetic connection between my feet and the soft soil. Although this seemed like a simple activity, it illuminated my inter-embrace with the earth. Mindfulness walking showed me that every step I take is a miracle to be grateful for.

I integrated mindfulness walks into my daily life. I tried not to be engrossed in the universe within my phone, and I walked through my neighborhood with curiosity and gratitude. I noticed so many things I had routinely overlooked. One day, during the summer, I returned to the monastery and eagerly embarked on the mindfulness walk. The group was much larger this time, and all thirty of us roamed around the forest and walked around the heart-shaped lake that had defrosted under the sun. There were so many beings that I had not noticed before. The forest floor was embedded with a carpet of soft, fluffy moss, and the trees were lush with unfurling leaves. I was so happy to be back, and I paid attention to the sensations that only the summertime generously provides.

In the middle of our walk, I looked to my right, and I saw a baby deer trotting right next to me. I gasped softly and expected the deer to quickly flee. Instead, he stayed and walked with us for the rest of the trail. He sensed our presence and wanted to share his presence with us too. It felt like such a rare and miraculous occurrence to move with each other at the same time. The monks told me that he routinely joined them on mindfulness walks and that they had named him Bamboo. Quiet tears started streaming down my face. I felt so moved by the profound interbeing of our lives.

Now, when I sit and meditate, I start with deep breathing. A deep inhale through the nose and a generous exhale through the mouth naturally slow down my beating heart. As my body naturally matches the pace of my breathing, the thoughts start to trickle in. Instead of shutting those thoughts down, I say to myself, "I am sitting, I am breathing, and I am thinking these thoughts with the present moment. This thought is part of my experience in this moment, and I sit with them until they pass." Becoming aware of what I am doing during sacred meditation allows me to become one with the moment. When I started practicing this way, I was no longer in a state of resistance, and I let those thoughts go. This awareness reverberates outside my meditative states and is channeled into every breath I take.

Every step and breath are blessings. When we practice presence, we exercise gratitude in everything we do. Our thankfulness echoes out into our everyday interactions: as we wake up in the mornings, during conversations with friends, and while listening to beautiful songs. When you take the time to savor stillness, you will notice all the ways that you move, and it will move you. You will see how your heart beats, your lungs expand, and your breath swirls, and it will be as charming and miraculous as a swaying weeping willow or a flock of soaring doves. When you sit in silence, you will notice the sounds that reverberate within you and beyond. You will hear the song of interconnection. You will realize that you are never alone.

I have learned of presence by sitting with plant kin. When I sit with plants or walk among them, their presence is deeply felt. They are full in their being as they grow toward the sun, sway in the breeze, and sleep with the stars. They are at peace in perpetual interconnection. Sometimes I shyly reach out and touch their unfurling leaves, petals, and fruits, and I am bewildered because every blossoming is a little miracle.

While I was at the peak of my pandemic depression, I read Robin Wall Kimmerer's book *Braiding Sweetgrass*. Kimmerer is a botanist, writer, and poet of the Citizen Potawatomi Nation of Turtle Island,* and she writes about Indigenous wisdom and the teachings of our plant relatives. She generously taught me so much about the interconnected relationships between us and plants, what it means to cultivate reciprocation and gratitude, and many fruitful possibilities in abundance and care. Not only did her book

---

*Turtle Island is the Indigenous name for the so-called United States of America. To learn about and acknowledge the Indigenous names of the places where you live, check out the app Native Land and the website native-land.ca.

teach me about relationships with Earth, but it also mended a fracture in my heart that was bleeding from my relationship with X.

In *Braiding Sweetgrass*, she wrote a moving chapter called "Asters and Goldenrod," about the natural attraction between yellow goldenrod flowers and purple aster flowers. During the springtime, you can find these yellow and purple flowers blooming next to each other everywhere you look. Kimmerer was so intrigued by this beautiful phenomenon that it propelled her to study botany. She wondered why beauty was so natural to Earth. She was dismissed by her white professor who told her that the question was irrelevant to a botanist's scientific studies. However, she sought guidance from her Indigenous elders and learned that the combination of the colors purple and yellow are most appealing to the human eye, and that these colors, in unison, also attract the eyes of bees. Not only do these yellow goldenrod flowers and purple aster flowers work together for their mutual survival, but they also sustain other living communities by providing food, pleasure, and beauty to us all. Her essay made me think about the inevitability of our interbeing, the beauty that comes from our many interconnections, and the intricacies that we do not notice when we fail to slow down.

To appreciate Earth and her many sacred connections, we must honor the Indigenous communities of the land. Indigenous people are the original caretakers of Earth and know what it means to be in interdependent and reciprocal relationship with the planet. A huge reason we might feel so disconnected, fragmented, and confused about climate change on Earth is because still, to this day, Indigenous communities are being violently displaced, erased, and silenced. Capitalism depreciates living beings as "resources" for extraction, and people are taught to see land as property for development. To experience true presence with miraculous Earth, we must remember why we feel so disconnected in the first place. Land is a sacred being we are in communion with, and we need to urgently shift our misguided ideas that regard land as property. We must be committed to giving land back to Indigenous communities, and urgently fight for Indigenous sovereignty.

After I finished reading *Braiding Sweetgrass*, I sat with it for a very long time. On lonely days, I would spend generous amounts of time just sitting with plants. I would sit under lemon trees and observe their ripening fruits, admire the way azalea flowers grow in abundant clusters, or watch a fern unfurl her leaves from tight little spirals. I noticed hummingbirds and bees suckle and bathe in nectar, lizards camouflage into the strong trunks of trees, and mushrooms peeking out from their cities of mycelium to greet us above the soil. I saw, in all this aliveness, my very own aliveness. I saw my survival, and how miraculous it was that I still got to experience communion on Earth. There are many reasons we find ourselves experiencing stark clarity when we go to the forest, the shore, or the desert. When I am present with my plant relatives, I realize that I am never alone. I am as multidimensional as Earth, and I am as soft as the soil I walk on. Whenever I meet my plant relatives, I meet myself. We were never separate to begin with.

The sea, the shore, and the sky all have their own relationships with time, and so does our healing. When I have sat with the presence of monks, flowers, moss, and baby deer, I have found myself uncovering deep-seated sensations. I am reminded of past lives, childhood memories, and moments of spiritual clarity in my life. Sometimes, during sunsets, I remember the sensations I felt when X and I watched the monarch butterfly migration in the Australian sunset. At every estuary, I recall the salty and fresh waters of Puerto Rico, which leads me down a path of childhood memories. Every time I meditate, I am linked to every grounding moment of presence in my life, and I think of Bamboo the baby deer guiding me through. When we experience true presence, our memories reveal their interconnected relationships with one another. We are not time-traveling but being welcomed into an amalgamation of past, present, and future.

When I am present with my hurt, all my heartbroken selves seem to meet and approach one another with curiosity and tenderness. As I reunite with every heartbroken version of myself it feels like they are all being reflected in a series of fun-house mirrors. What did we learn this time? Similar lessons about addiction, codependence, performance, and validation reemerge with the ghosts from my past. At the core of all my heartbreaks reverberates a loud resounding truth: I have been so committed to finding my presence in other relationships that I had forgotten to nurture my relationship with myself. I know now that the generosity of heartbreak serves as an invitation to get to know exactly how lovable we are for ourselves.

While I have met many heartbroken selves, I have also reunited with many joyous versions of me. I link arms with versions of myself who heal in heartbreak, who went to the ocean for guidance, who wrote expressively in letters and journals, and who cried and danced for sweet release. I met my many loving selves, the ones who adamantly insisted that I not abandon my existence. I reminisce on moments of presence that I have experienced on my own, in the vastness of deserts, in lush forests surrounded by trees, and in bed with the sun. I think of all the sacred relationships I am a part of, and the relationships I have had with myself. I have experienced so much joy despite my many heartbreaks, and though I have not always engaged in healthy coping mechanisms, I have always been open to learning and healing. I was always committed to life.

With presence, I have met myself wholly again. In each mindful step, I have extended a hand to all my past selves. Instead of shelving them in the binaries of past and present, I look at myself as a culmination of all of them. I embody millions of moments, as they all gather like stardust to create an embodied universe. As I am present, I can strengthen the interconnected miracles that connect us all. When I meet all my multitudes, I realize that they have all always been there, waiting for me to notice them. No doubt, it feels like I am falling in love again. I am in love with myself and everything that I am inseparable from.

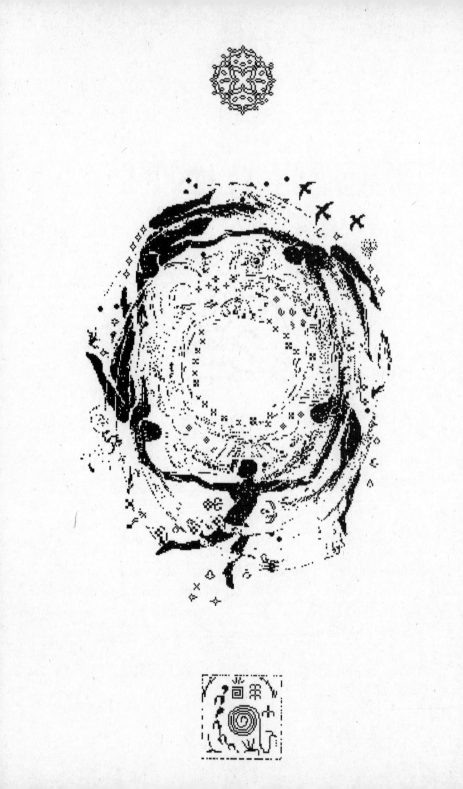

EIGHT

COMMUNITY

A Chorus of Belonging

I hear the clatter of cymbals and drums, and I am surrounded by friends, children, families, and elders. I am at a queer Lunar New Year party* in New York City. There is free food, vibrant decorations, and an exciting lineup of performances by intergenerational members of the diasporic Asian community. The upbeat clamor of traditional Chinese festive music rings through the air, and I am eagerly awaiting the ancestral lion dance performance.† The dance begins, and three colorful lions emerge onstage. They are lavished in glorious golden swirls and fuzzy

---

*This party was hosted by Wing On Wo, Yellow Jackets Collective, and Abrons Arts Center.

†The performance was by the Wan Chi Ming Hung Gar Institute Dragon and Lion Dance Team.

trimming, and underneath the lion costume you can see pairs of scurrying feet. The lions jump atop bamboo shoots, humorously engulf entire heads of lettuce, and unravel scrolls that wish us a wonderful year of abundance.

During the performance, I have an out-of-body experience. While watching the lions and the crowd, I am also watching myself absorbed in awe. From a bird's-eye view, I see that I am a part of something big, and it feels as if my being were synthesizing with all the scents, sounds, and sights around me. I am moved by the movement that I see, and my spirit moves, too, vibrating and extending. Something profoundly spiritual is activated and reveals a pearl of wisdom that is precious and innate: I am experiencing the bliss of belonging. I have longed for this kind of communion for so long, where queer and trans people of color could feel safe and joyful in our complex cultures, aunties and uncles could feel excited and unashamed in their remembrance, and children could learn about their ancestors and themselves. I say wow out loud while tears begin to fall, and my excitement amalgamates with the beauty of intergenerational communion.

While I listen to all the sprightly surrounding sounds, I think of the convergence of our many different songs. There is the sound of children's laughter, lively applause, oohs and aahs of admiration, and the constant clanging of a gong. We all sing our different tunes, though I hear our harmonies coalescing. My wows merge with the music and create melodies that I often dreamed of as a lonely child. This beautiful event felt like a homecoming where the spiritual barriers between us could come crashing down. The sound of communion is when my tune merges with yours, unfolding into an infinite intergenerational song. It has taken me a long time to find it, but I can hear it now.

Even though X and I spent most of our time together during our relationship, I always felt alone. X encouraged me to disconnect from everyone around me and manipulated me into believing that it was us against the world. He would say things like "Nobody will love you like I do" and talk about how rare our connection was. As our bubble grew suffocatingly small, it was difficult to nurture relationships outside of ours. I started to believe that I existed to serve X, and that our relationship was the only opportunity of love that I would ever experience. So I grasped our connection with all the energy that I could muster, and I was terrified of our demise because I was fearful of being alone. Without him, I thought that I had no other connection with the world.

When I was young, I was sold a dream of romance. Mainstream pop culture fed me idyllic visions of Technicolor relationships that consisted of cis-heterosexual couples running away together, building homes, having children, and staying in their small nuclear bubbles of love. I was not taught the importance of community, and in these domestic pipe dreams, close relationships were bound by either genetics or marriage. My parents had been sold the same dream, and they had worked hard to maintain that image. What pop culture never told us was the consequences of said domestic isolation, and I had to see for myself what happened behind closed doors. Within my tight nuclear family, our relationships were riddled with loneliness and trauma. We felt so isolated in suburban white Australia that it seemed as if we could turn only to one another, even when we were causing one another sorrow. As I grew older, I subconsciously replicated those dynamics in my relationship with X. I cowered, and X controlled, and I stayed because I did not want to abandon the dream. I thought that leaving relationships was a form of failure, and I stayed until our relationship was a waking nightmare.

When we feel isolated, it is easier for us to be controlled. When our worlds seem small, our yearning for belonging can be manipulated. X shrunk my world because he did not want me to see the abundance of possibilities that awaited me. He was fearful of my freedom and used a mindset of scarcity to light a flame of fear within. When our relationship ended, I felt lost, and I had become so self-isolated that I did not know who to turn to.

If we zoom out to a societal scale, we see that oppressive fascist states employ their own abusive tactics to isolate us from one another. They plant seeds of fear by severing our togetherness because they deeply fear a people's resistance. They teach us to confine ourselves to isolated domesticity so that our connections are fractured, and use fear to prevent us from collectively finding creative alternatives to the restrictive lessons we've been taught. They want to prevent us from seeing the possibilities that our interconnected relationships hold. It is profound and beautiful when human beings converge, experiment, and connect in our togetherness, and people who try to police those spaces only do so because they know how powerful community can be. They are afraid, and they want us to be afraid of ourselves. I believe those people are lost, and that they, too, seek deep belonging but are too afraid to admit it.

We live in a culture where heteronormative romantic love is hierarchized as the most desired relationship, actively deeming queer relationships, community, and friendship as inferior, and excluding other forms of love, connection, and intimacy. I internalized this hierarchy and placed my romantic relationships on pedestals, while simultaneously deprioritizing all my other relationships. In this hierarchy, community took a back seat. I began to disregard community as only necessary for the fun, shallow, indulgent side of life, and I was sorely misinformed on what community could look like. I could not even begin to fathom the possibilities of platonic intimacy, romantic friendships, or nonmonogamous romance. When my relationship with X finally ended, I felt overwhelmingly lost because I had become so self-isolated and did not know where else to turn. I had no choice but to relearn my ideas of love because it became very apparent to me that the isolating and heteronormative standards were not working. I did not see it at the time, but as our relationship ended, along came abundant openings.

On the night that X assaulted me in the Oakland alleyway, I watched my brief life flash before my eyes. That night when I escaped, I also experienced communion at its most powerful. My friends mobilized quickly as they took care of me, caressed me, held me, dressed my wounds, and helped me decipher my feelings. They promised me protection and supported me while I was vulnerable, betrayed, and hurt. They did not force me to "get better" or dictate my path to healing, and as they saw me teeter on the edge of an emotional cliff, they ran to catch me when I fell. My friends showed me love amid the most horrific of circumstances. The way my friends held me was an embodiment of the love that I was searching for, but never found, in X.

While unlearning the heteronormative standards of romance and family, I realized that my biological and romantic relationships were not always the safest spaces for love. As much as we may love our biological families, there are dimensions of our identities that we may not feel safe exploring with them. We cannot choose which families we are born into, and some people, especially queer and trans people, have families that are abusive or demanding or unaccepting. Just because we experience difficulties with our biological families does not mean that we will never experience kinship. Being in community allows us to relearn love by redefining what a family can be.

I relearned love slowly by listening to my own intuition. When X and I were over, I felt immensely fragile, anxious, and timid. I carried with me a whirlwind of feelings and fragments of my identity that I was never allowed to explore. I slowly started to open up to my friends about how heartbroken and ashamed I was. I was dedicated to releasing that shame by being honest with myself, and so I started talking to myself as if I were an infant and learning the art of reparenting. I listened to my most basic needs from the voice of my inner child and learned how to cater to them. I allowed myself to break down and show immense vulnerability, and I asked myself how I felt in public spaces, knowing that X might be nearby. I listened to myself whimper in fear and sob uncontrollably. I listened to those needs, and after some time and consideration, I chose an act of love that required me to put some space between me and my familiar surroundings. I decided to move to New York.

Moving to New York was both exciting and full of struggle. I had no job prospects, and I knew only a few people in the city. After some unstable housing situations, I was invited to live in a queer cooperative household* with ten other queer people of color. Upon moving in, I knew only one of them.† The intention of the house was clear: we wanted to create a space for queer and trans people of color that was safe from white supremacy and queerphobia, and that allowed us to live new experimental dreams of communal living, chosen family, and queer love. We all grew extremely close. We shared extravagant potluck meals, traveled together in a huge collective, and held one another during times of hardship. We watched one another fall in and out of love, stretch outside our comfort zones, live our dreams, and learn crucial life lessons. During the harshest of winters, we would prepare warm meals for one another and cuddle in the freezing night. We loved one another in ways that dismantled my learned ideas of heteronormative romantic partnership, and we explored intimacy in tender and nonconsumptive ways. Committing to queer love meant allowing safe spaces for our oscillating, ever-changing, ever-fluid, multifaceted identities.

Of course, there was ample conflict. We argued and bickered and disagreed. Sometimes our arguments would trigger us and remind us of painful family dynamics. Now and then, we became codependent, because our chosen family became so close that we did not know how to spend time without one another. We were challenged to set distinct boundaries and learned that boundaries,

---

*Shout-out to the Queer World.

†With love to my friend Nuur, who introduced me to an entire world of queer love.

too, are acts of love. When I reflect on those times, I often think of somatics practitioner Prentis Hemphill's* reflection "Boundaries are the distance at which I can love you and me simultaneously." We were rediscovering family and making new choices that we were unable to make as queer children.

At times we were seeking perfection, in hopes that the queer household would be free of any harm that we were familiar with. When our household did not feel like utopia, some of us would take it personally, as if we had failed one another and ourselves. We would punish one another, call one another names, and reenact the same harm that we had experienced in past relationships. Expecting utopia didn't take into consideration how complicated and layered each of us was, and how, as queer people of color, we have all endured and survived traumatic experiences. Our traumatized projections leaked into our arguments, and as much as we held one another, we hurt one another too.

Yet even during the rockiest periods of our togetherness, we still vowed to support one another in ways that we knew. Whenever I experienced a mental health crisis, financial instability, or immigration struggles, my chosen family would mobilize to make sure that I had the resources I needed, and that, most important, I felt safe and protected. I vowed to do the same for them. In many ways, we were all able to access our inner children together, and we spoke to one another as if we were babies and provided for one another with our own unique gifts. I felt safe exploring my queerest freakiest self and was even encouraged and celebrated for it. These were new euphoric feelings, and I learned what it felt like to be loved as a whole and dynamic person. To be non-white and

---

*Check out Prentis Hemphill's podcast *Finding Our Way*.

queer means to be in constant resistance to ways in which mainstream cultures are designed to thrive. We defined our own survival and supported one another in our mutual strength, in hopes that one day we would not have to be in active resistance anymore. We hoped that one day soon we could just be. We embarked on that together, through all the nuance and conflict and intimacy and celebration, and I learned of closeness not so much as striving for perfection, but of collectively finding our way.

Perhaps being in community isn't as much about creating a utopia as it is about allowing space for complexity and celebrating those meeting places. When we are in communion, we create millions of unique points that dot the sky in shimmering constellations. We dance around one another like shining mirrors and watch how all our pain and our joys combine. At our most joyful, we experience moments of synthesis. At our messiest, we are given raw opportunities to learn and unlearn many complexities, and to guide one another and ourselves in an intertwining process. Through meaningful relationships we are forced to be honest with ourselves and one another, and that is an act of love. We are taught how to set boundaries, hold ourselves accountable, heal interdependently, and communicate effectively in myriad ways. Being human is ever complex and being queer means to be in perpetual metamorphosis. In communion, we hold one another through fear and emerge from it in rapturous song and dance.

That dark night in Oakland, my friends' commitment to care showed me kinship in new and urgent ways. It jolted me to rid myself of the hierarchies I had been bound to and propelled me toward a journey of nourishing and queering my chosen relationships. My friends allowed me to be vulnerable in their arms, wiping my tears and assuring me that they would love me even as my unpredictable and messy emotions came to the surface. They did not wish to control me, nor were they threatened by the honest displays of my emotion. As they massaged my hands and my feet, I learned that loving communion is finding new ways of sharing safety and ensuring mutual liberation. Finding people who honor your full multidimensional self is not easy, but when you do, you have begun relearning love, and you have found chosen family.

Growing up in a lower-middle-class Asian household meant that I was raised with a scarcity mindset. My parents had to work much harder than most of the white people around them, and their dreams were constantly invalidated or seen as a threat. Anytime our family would experience a bout of good fortune, we would immediately fear that we would lose it all. My mother would hoard supplies and buy anything that was on sale, even if we did not need it. We were convinced that we had to hold on tight to the blessings because we thought that we would never get as lucky again. We did not think that we could receive more. My scarcity mindset became so severe that sometimes I would not even eat the last bite of my food, in order to savor it and make it last. Eventually, the last of my food would rot, and nobody would get to enjoy it. My family was so afraid of losing our blessings that our fear eclipsed our ability to enjoy them.

Much of our scarcity seemed to come from loneliness. As our

home became tight and insulated, my parents rarely had guests or friends over. We lived in a white neighborhood and did not share much in common with our neighbors. Our only friends were a Samoan Chinese family we had known since I was a child, but we rarely saw one another because we were always working. The isolation within our nuclear family created tension and triggered our projections. My parents went out in public and were yelled at because English was their second language. We would deal with ridicule and humiliation, and then come home and scream at one another. White people watched us with a suspicious gaze, and because of that we shrunk ourselves, and our hopes for abundance shrunk too.

Our yearning for belonging is an extremely natural desire, and it is beautiful to see the possibilities that human beings conjure when we come together. Unfortunately, our sense of belonging is also seen as a threat. Our desire for togetherness disrupts the hyper-individualistic capitalist agenda that asks us to strive for the house with the high fences, pine for the gated communities, and protect the private properties where we will not be "disturbed." The people who are adamant about preserving hierarchies are often the very same people who are stewing in loneliness themselves. Communion is foreign to them because they have based their existence on distancing themselves from their fellow beings, and being in community disrupts the competition that they have dedicated their lives to. They teach us to form relationships not for the sake of communion, but for the sake of consumption. Not only do we consume one another, but we also consume ourselves. How do we find belonging then, when it feels like we no longer belong to our bodies?

Being in community is like nourishing a garden. Gardens are abundant places full of a diversity of beings that are in communion with one another. Sometimes different plants in our gardens encourage others' growth and provide shade, protection, and nutrients. Sometimes plants suffocate one another or compete for light and food. In a garden, you can witness many forms of reciprocation, communication, and conflict. There, you can learn what it means to be in community with human beings and nonhuman beings alike.

Annika Hansteen-Izora is a designer and writer who suggests that community is an abundant ecosystem. In their writing, they explore the idea that we could be in a communal learning garden, in which we learn how to be in community with one another. They ponder, "Can we fight for each other to ensure we can all access these ecosystems, that we can bring our full selves, boundaries and needs? Can we more deeply connect the dots between our individual passions and local, national and world actions against dominations?"*

Gardens teach me that abundance is multiplied by relationships. In the springtime, when I watch the bees bounce in fluffy beds of pollen, I get to witness a reciprocal becoming. As the bees guarantee the survival of their kin, they also nourish the flowers that they pollinate. Gardens strengthen relationships between species, including the relationships that human beings have with one another and with Earth. In a garden, all the trees, flowers, and insects are

---

*Check out Annika's wonderful work at their website, annikaizora.com.

singing their intertwining songs. When we dance together in synchronicity and euphoria, it feels like we are sunflowers swaying in the breeze, not competing, but sharing and basking in the sun.

In *Braiding Sweetgrass*, Robin Wall Kimmerer shares a profound lesson from our plant siblings about relationships of reciprocation. She writes about the Three Sisters Harvest, which is an Indigenous tradition of planting together the Three Sisters: corn, squash, and beans. In the spring, all Three Sisters are planted at the same time. Once the seeds are in the fertile ground, the corn will be the first to shoot up from the soil. The tall cornstalks lend themselves as stable structures for the beans, which climb up the cornstalks and joyfully greet the sun. The sun's nutrients move into the beans' roots, and the beans work their magic underground by transforming atmospheric nitrogen to mineral nitrogen, which they share with the rest of their sisters. Then, slowly, finally, the squash spread their broad leaves out from the soil. The squash leaves remain close to the ground and act as umbrellas, providing shade and allowing the soil to retain moisture so that all Three Sisters can remain hydrated. The Three Sisters flourish, and they do so because they uplift and support one another's growth.

Robin Wall Kimmerer shares the wisdoms of the Three Sisters with us:

Of all the wise teachers who have come into my life, none are more eloquent than these, who wordlessly in leaf and vine embody the knowledge of relationship. Alone, a bean is just a vine, squash an oversize leaf. Only when standing together with corn does a whole emerge which transcends the individual. The gifts of each are more fully expressed when they are nurtured together than alone. In ripe ears and swelling fruit, they counsel us that all gifts are multiplied in relationship. This is how the world keeps going.

The Three Sisters are our teachers, and they show us what it means to be in true communion. Can we learn from the Three Sisters in their kinship and cooperation? Can we apply that to our relationships today?

We are all part of a garden, and we can only flourish if we embrace all our dimensions. Like the Three Sisters, the survival of all of us is important, and we need one another to thrive. We all have unique talents, interests, passions, and gifts that will allow us to provide for ourselves and one another. We also have varying levels of privilege and access that need to be redistributed with transparency. The Three Sisters enact a language of reciprocity that we need to become fluent in. Reciprocity is a perpetual exchanging of gifts that allows us to see the abundance that should be available to us all. Our networks are as intricate as the communities that grow in the earth, and as we explore our interconnections, we need to nourish our soil. We cannot be a sibling without a family, we cannot be a seed without a garden, we cannot be in communion without community, and we cannot be human without Earth. We cannot know of love without one another, so let us learn together.

I was extremely lucky to have found chosen family even when I did not have access to wealth. I moved to New York with very little money, and it is because of our communal living that we were able to divide cheap rent, share food stamps, and support one another in times of crisis. We made it a priority to ensure that our dynamics did not feel exclusive, and we welcomed queer and trans people of color who needed places to stay. However, I want to acknowledge that not all survivors have the privilege or resources to leave the abusive homes and relationships that they are trapped in. There are limitations to resources such as talk therapy and holistic healing, and that it is deeply important for survivors to first and foremost have access to basic material needs, such as safe housing, clothing, and food. This brings me back to how important it is to acknowledge our various privileges and how we can ensure that we are redistributing the resources that we have access to. While I sit with gratitude for the blessings that I received in New York, I must ask myself critical questions: How can I share and multiply these blessings? How am I actively extending that network of support? How can I try my best to ensure that all survivors get a chance and a choice to experience community, chosen family, and true love?

I am grateful for grassroots organizations that hold me accountable to these questions. I am grateful for mutual aid, crowdfunding, and survivor-centered resources. Grassroots organizations and collectives in New York City taught me most of what I know about queer community and mutual aid. BUFU,* which stands for By Us For Us, is a collective led by four queer Black and Asian organizers. They created the BUFU Summer School and invited queer people of color all over the city to join, teach, and learn about mutual aid. They invited everybody to bring their own wisdoms and skills and insisted that we were all teachers as much as

---

*Check out BUFU's work at their website bufubyusforus.com.

we were students. During the COVID-19 pandemic, BUFU and China Residencies collaborated with community members all over the world to create Cloud 9,* which is an extensive online directory that lists international and US-specific resources for housing, food, financial assistance, spiritual guidance, holistic medicine, education, grief support, and online community.

Radical Love Consciousness is a queer Black- and Asian-led collective that also deeply radicalized me.† Before the COVID-19 pandemic, they held classes, fundraisers, clothing swaps, and movie screenings all year round for people who were seeking community amid the swift rhythms of the city. Neema Githere, one of the members of the collective, deeply ingrained in us the spirit of radical love by facilitating classes that allowed us to hold difficult conversations and learn what love looks like in praxis. They taught us that "reparations must be interpersonal and ongoing," and that the honest redistribution of our resources must be a commitment in our everyday lives.

The term "mutual aid" was first documented in Western academia in the late 1800s. In 1902, Pyotr Kropotkin wrote a book called *Mutual Aid: A Factor of Evolution*, exploring ideas of mutual aid that were based on his observation of animals and their communities. In his writings, he rejected Darwinist claims that all species are in competition with one another for survival. Instead, he observed that our sense of solidarity is deep, intuitive, and ingrained.

While that was the first acknowledgment of mutual aid in recorded Western history, I wish to point out that these archives do

---

*You can find the resource guide at cloud9.support.

†Support their work and sign up on their membership platform at patreon.com/radicallove.

not adequately trace the history of reciprocation in action back to its origins. The emergence of Darwinism erased many Indigenous wisdoms that were rooted in mutual aid, cooperation, and interdependence. Relationships of reciprocity have existed since the beginning of life, and many historical forms of Indigenous mutual aid were destroyed by colonization. There are many undocumented chronicles of mutual aid, including oral histories, that we must neither forget nor erase. Many Indigenous-led collectives, such as Seeding Sovereignty* and Weaving Our Paths,† are doing ongoing mutual aid work today, and we must be grateful for the Indigenous communities who have always understood that community is an interspecies, intergenerational, interconnected necessity of life.

In *Sand Talk: How Indigenous Thinking Can Save the World*, the wisdoms of Aboriginal writer Tyson Yunkaporta perfectly summarize the ethics at the root of mutual aid, where we denounce the need for competition and instead commit to understanding the material resources and gifts that we can share with one another.

> It is difficult to relinquish the illusions of power and delusions of exceptionalism that come with privilege. But it is strangely liberating to realize your true status as a single node in a cooperative network. There is honor to be found in this role, and a certain dignified agency. You won't be swallowed up by a hive mind

---

*My friends at Seeding Sovereignty do incredible work in decolonizing education and creating Land Back initiatives such as their Ancestral Acres Farm & Garden. Check out their work at seedingsovereignty.org.

†Weaving Our Paths is a network of "Queer, Trans, Two Spirit, Gender Non Conforming, Black, Indigenous, People of Color leaders, artists, organizers, mobilizers, and visionaries" whose work you can support at weavingour paths.life.

or lose your individuality—you will retain your autonomy while simultaneously being profoundly interdependent and connected.

All over the world, there is a lack of adequate health care, monetary support, education, and food. During the COVID-19 pandemic, in the United States, there was a severe lack of health and food resources for working-class communities of color, especially Black, Indigenous, immigrant, and disabled people. Many communities needed to take matters into their own hands. Mariame Kaba wrote a guide with the hashtag #wegotourblock* that was specific to neighborhood mutual aid, breaking down the steps that it takes to build a strong mutual aid network: for example, inviting neighbors to join your network, building pods by setting up different lines of communication, and getting to know one another's varying needs for material and nonmaterial resources, such as food, childcare, medicine, financial support, emotional support, language translation, tech assistance, and timely information.

In Brooklyn, there was an emergence of community fridges† and free food pantries created by local organizers from Playground Coffee Shop.‡ The Herbal Mutual Aid Network§ distributes free herbs and plant-based healing remedies to Black people in need

---

*You can check out Mariame Kaba's mutual aid guide at resources.mutualaid.nyc/services/826893620571128.

†You can find a map of community fridges all over New York City at nycfridge.com.

‡Playground Coffee Shop was founded by Zenat Begum; check out their work at playgroundcoffeeshop.com.

§HMAN was founded by Yves B. Golden and Remy Maelen; you can give or receive plant-based care via their website hman.love/.

of support. Guanábana* started a community library that asked people to take and leave books. For the Gworls† is a Black trans-led collective that continues to fundraise to pay for rent and gender-affirming surgeries for Black trans people. CAAAV‡ is an organization that works to promote housing justice and builds grassroots empowerment for working-class Asian immigrant communities in New York City. All these organizations are deeply creative in their extensions of care, and they taught me that because abusive systems do not provide for us, we must provide for one another.§

Leah Lakshmi Piepzna-Samarasinha wrote an article titled "How Disabled Mutual Aid Is Different Than Abled Mutual Aid"¶ for the Disability Visibility Project. It is important to note that while many abled people were introduced to mutual aid during the COVID-19 pandemic, disabled communities have been engaging in mutual aid for a very long time. The article details their personal experience during the COVID-19 pandemic as a disabled person, and they share some disabled mutual aid networks that worked hard to make sure that immunocompromised people were taking care of one another during quarantine.

---

*Guanábana was founded by Duneska Suannette Michel; find out more about their events, book clubs, and community library via Instagram: instagram.com/guanabana.nyc.

†To apply for various assistance programs, visit For the Gworls's website at forthegworls.party/home.

‡Explore CAAAV's important intergenerational organizing work at caaav.org.

§Most of the organizations I mentioned are based in Lenapehoking (New York City) because I live there and am most familiar with the organizing circles in that area.

¶You can read the article online at disabilityvisibilityproject.com/2021/10/03/how-disabled-mutual-aid-is-different-than-abled-mutual-aid.

But there were many other mutual aid groups I have heard of that seemed to not think about disabled people or ableism at all—as people who wanted to organize, as people other than faceless recipients of care—who also seemed to be ignorant of the specifically ableist and racist histories of charities and how those dynamics could easily creep into mutual aid. I wasn't ever sure if they were talking about us and it seemed strange that disabled people were never mentioned. Not only were they not thinking about ableism, they seemed to talk about "mutual aid" without ever referencing that sick and disabled people had been practicing it for years, that there might be something (or like, a lot) to learn from us, and that a pandemic was a disabled event. Or that the term "collective care" was invented by radical disabled women and nonbinary people of color who were and [are] part of the disability justice movement.

It is important to remember that it is inherently harmful to think of mutual aid as a form of charity. Charity depends on a hierarchy of power and asks people to inherit a power-over savior complex. Mutual aid is not the opportunity for a privileged able-bodied wealthy white person to feel like a hero for their "allyship." We need to be critical about who is typically included and excluded when we talk about community. While we are engaging in community work, I call on all of us to ask whether our work is consistently anti-racist, anti-ableist, anti-transphobic, anti-classist, and intergenerational. It is crucial to always reflect on the systemic inequities and imbalances that violently affect people's lives. By considering all these things, we strengthen our relationships and rebuild a sense of trust.

Engaging in mutual aid is committing to an ongoing redistribution of resources, tapping into our ingrained sense of solidarity, demanding equity in an unjust society, and imagining the infinite possibilities of what is to come. It is creating clear calls to action, organizing with intention, setting firm boundaries, and moving through the inevitability of conflict. Mutual aid honors our unique differences, gifts, talents, and passions, while discerning our privileges to figure out how to share and multiply abundance. We keep one another warm, we make sure everybody is fed, and we try our best to ensure safe and accountable spaces. We do so in perpetuity, and not exclusively during times of crisis. Communion is part of the foundations of creation, imagination, and life, and shows us that we can create abundance from care.

There is a park I like to go to in Brooklyn, in a neighborhood that is home to large Asian and Latinx communities. Each summer, I have gone to the park at sunset to watch the sky turn tangerine. Every day without fail, a group of Chinese aunties begin to dance. The group would slowly grow and expand as the sun turned red. Eventually, there would be not only Chinese women but people of all races and ages, coming together to participate in communal movement. Grandparents held hands with their grandchildren and most people recognized one another and caught up in meaningful conversations. I heard Chinese aunties joyfully chatting in

Cantonese, talking about their children, and complaining about the heat. The circle would become wider, the movements stronger, and the synchronized clapping louder. It was hard to trace who was choreographing the dance moves because everybody followed one another in a ripple effect: if you clapped, I clapped. There was a sense of trust in this togetherness. Sometimes I joined in; other times I would sit and watch, profoundly moved.

I do not want to fetishize or romanticize the life of any person, no matter what identities we share. I cannot imagine our complex individual experiences, though I can witness with awe the communal joy we share when we find one another. In the dance circles I saw huge grins, mutual recognition, and an intimate sense of trust. I do not know how many people knew one another, but what I did see was that people were not deeming the space exclusive or limited to anyone. People were not afraid, and people wanted to be together. Anybody could spontaneously join in and bring their energy to the collective movement. More energy birthed more joy. I saw, quite literally before my eyes, community multiplying in abundance.

I wondered about my family and how different it would have been if we had been surrounded by neighbors who shared food, meals, language, and culture with us. I wondered how different it would have been if we could have heard music outside our windows, people chattering in their dialects, and a coming together of cultures and stories. Our obsession with private property creates spiritual barriers, and my family would have felt a lot less lonely if we had felt welcomed by all our neighbors. When we immerse ourselves in our ever-expanding circles, our abundance grows because we share our gifts. There is not a finite supply of joy, but an infinite multiplying of the music of love. And so, we dance.

When we are together, we create infinite possibilities, not just for our survival but also for our ever-expanding abundance. Our dance circles expand every time we come together, and our togetherness is perceived as a threat precisely because it is so powerful. Our songs become louder, and our voices become stronger in unison. Communion is a sacred form of presence, and it is only threatening to those who cannot admit to themselves that they yearn for it. In togetherness, I abandon the ideas of an isolated individual self, and am reminded that my love is connected to all love. As I dance, you dance. As I sing, you sing, and my blossoming is your blossoming.

NINE

MIRACLE

The Miracle in Being

When we think of miracles, we often think of huge, unexplainable events that bring us immeasurable blessings. We think of the heavenly, the godly, and the superstitious. It feels miraculous when we fall in love, when our lives are saved from danger, and when we achieve what we thought was impossible. I believe in miracles of every scale, though I know that there are miracles that I have often overlooked. I want to honor the miracles that might be seen as small and that exist as brief and passing moments. I wish to honor the miracles that we carry as we wake and sleep each day. Every sunset is a miracle, and so is every breath.

I have cried during many sunsets, each one a miraculous display of transition and irreverence. I have traveled to reach the top of a hill, the steep edge of a cliff, and the end of a shore, just to watch the sun descend. No matter how many times I have watched this spectacle, I never grow tired of seeing a sunset's splendor. I am most moved when I watch a sunset in solitude, and I look beside me and see somebody else doing the same. They are usually silent and in awe, or they are taking photographs or making a video call to a loved one to share and remember this moment. I cannot imagine what lingers in this other person's thoughts and dreams, though I am grateful for the time we took, together and apart, to honor such a sacred moment in our day. We never know what each sunset will look like, and we anticipate it with bated breath, struck by colors we never even realized existed. At every moment of the day, somebody is watching the sun rise or set, and that makes me weep.

Noticing the miracles around us is deep inner-child work. It allows us to reconnect with our childlike curiosities. As a lonely child, I was delighted by almost everything, especially anything that signified life. I raised caterpillars into butterflies, ran around in the rain, and was incredulous at the "crunch" of falling leaves. I asked so many questions, and my wows were loud and boisterous. Slowly, as I grew older, I adopted a dissatisfaction and disdain toward life. I became disenchanted by Earth and drew my attention away from my surroundings and deep into the matrix of the digital world. A bitterness engulfed my spirit as I grew familiar with ugly truths, and all the things I was amazed by did not seem to receive much recognition from society. After a while, it felt as if the only miracles that were acknowledged were the man-made ones. When did Earth stop being miraculous to us, and when did we stop noticing her splendor? When did we experience the dimming of our wows?

Each sunrise and sunset is a miracle, and we are spoiled with the pleasure of experiencing them every day. If we begin to think of miracles as everyday occurrences, we could notice them all around us, and maybe even within ourselves. Perhaps then we could see miracles on micro levels, and revel in the delight that they have a constant presence in our lives. Seeing miracles every day does not take away from the grand and unexplainable but expands our ideas of what miracles can be: every blossom of a flower, every push and pull of the tide, every time we breathe in, and every time we breathe out. If we reignited our curiosities, we could see that miracles are the fabric of our very existence.

Curiosity is conditioned out of so many of us from an early age. We have our first encounters with death and violence, and we are taught various ways to "grow up" to survive in cruel conditions and serve a societal purpose. We are quickly told that our existence is simply not enough, and that we must work and fight for basic needs and goodness. Our curiosity is deemed useless, trivial, and meant for children, and we are taught that there is no room left for wonder. We are given strict guidelines to stick to the status quo to become productive parts of society and obtain joy, as if happiness were a product we could purchase. We become enticed by the universes that we see through our blue screens, and we become so convinced by these simulations of living that we forget how to live. In the digital age, we are torn in so many directions, pulled toward a realm that begs us to consume more and notice less.

On the subway, I see so many ducked heads and arched backs staring at their screens, and nobody notices the subway performers playing their beautiful songs. If we simply looked up, we would see so much. Without our curiosity, there is so much that we forget, and we become absent in our everyday lives. Realizing the precious nature of each passing moment reveals not only that you have survived, but that you continue to live.

It was difficult to believe in anything as miracle after surviving my relationship with X. In the thickness of my grief, I wanted to die. I could barely sleep or eat, let alone work and socialize, and my movements were as minimal as I could muster. The only thing that mattered was that I got through another day. What I could do was sit with myself and stare out the window, and when I found the strength, I took myself on short strolls close to home. I noticed crisp leaves falling, uproarious choruses from an orchestra of cicadas, and sweet and salty scents all around. When I did, I accessed a vulnerability that had been muted long ago, and I noticed a lot more around me. In this fragile and precarious state, all of my senses were heightened, and my curiosity was coming back.

Sometimes on my walks, I would see couples embracing, and while at first it felt like a stab to the heart, I became so moved because I was reminded that even in my hopelessness, love was all around. It did not have to be "mine," but it was still connected to me. I felt lucky to bear witness to love. I watched floating clouds, swaying trees, and streams of sunbeams dancing with the day, and I felt immensely moved because I realized that I shared life with all the small miracles around me. In the healing of my heartbreak, I began to see the miracle within me, too, inseparable, inevitable, and intertwined. At what felt like the precipice of death, I was reminded of my miraculous life, and I was reborn.

In our lifetimes, I think that we are reborn many times. While I may not remember my initial arrival from my mother's womb, I recall many resurrections. Most of the time, they came after pain-stricken periods of heartbreak and grief, when it was difficult to continue. However, in my continuance, my curiosity returned, and my wonder widened. My curiosity was especially heightened when I strengthened my relationship with Earth. Some days I sat by the ocean to see how each wave paralleled the deep rhythms of my own breath. Sometimes I would watch the rain as it replenished Earth and relieved her of a drought, and I saw how each raindrop mirrored every tear that I have shed. Anytime that I could, I watched the setting sun in her brilliant continuance as she reenacted the rebirth of each passing day.

The word "miracle" is technically defined as a noun, but what if we thought of a miracle as an action? In the same way that bell hooks describes love as a verb, what if we believed that we are engaging in miracle as a movement, and that we are constantly miracle-ing with every sacred breath? If we believed, as we grow from children into adults, that every single breath we take is an enactment of miracle making, then perhaps we could see life as a gift instead of something we must prove ourselves worthy of. What would shift in our world if we believed in ourselves as living miracles?

As I accessed my childlike curiosity and wonder, I was wowed by the life that surrounded me. While what I observed may not be regarded as particularly grand or exciting, I was bewildered by some of the sights and sounds that sharpened with my perspective.

I allowed myself to behold the sky, and as I cloud-gazed, I realized how often I forgot about the shifting nature of the world above. In fact, I had forgotten that Earth is in constant rotation and that she moves with everything that lives with her. There are so many preliminary questions that we ask as children like "Why is the sky blue?" or "Why is the grass green?" because we are confounded by pure splendor. As we grow older, we are discouraged from asking those questions because they are deemed simple, obvious, or unimportant. Recently, I realized that I still did not know a lot of the answers, so I started asking them again.

I remember how most of the answers to the questions I posed as a child were presented to me scientifically. I was fascinated by these intricate scientific facts and findings, though I was also a little dissatisfied with how disenchanted my teachers were. It almost seemed as if some of them wanted to reduce the wonder of nature to unimaginative statistics. They would often explain that this was just how the world worked, and that there was no magical reason as to why the grass is green or the sky is blue—they were simply part of mechanical, functional, and logical ecosystems that sustain species' survival. Despite my teachers' mundane delivery, I still found myself thinking, *That is magical too!* The mysteries of the universe might have been translated into science, but that does not make them any less miraculous or magnificent. Maybe there are no accurate answers to our questions, for there are some secrets too precious to the universe for us to ever know.

What if we taught our children that every question that they ask is miraculous in itself? What if we taught them that every blink and breath are an indication of life and therefore an active form of miracle-ing? Children have taught me so much about the wisdoms of wonder. One evening at sunset, I was walking with my neighbor and her three-year-old daughter and saw how the little girl pointed up at every pink cloud in the sky. In the corner of her eye, she would sense the presence of a bird or a bug, greet them, and exclaim in sheer joy and excitement. She knew the name of everyone in the neighborhood, and she would wave at people without feeling shy. Her curiosity was contagious and heightened all my senses. I hope that she experiences the same kind of glee when she looks in the mirror, and she sees herself as flourishing and wise as the flowers. I hope that she can see that her continuance, her movement, and her bountiful curiosity are gifts to the universe. I hope we all do.

One of the people who encouraged my curiosity was my late grandfather. We always asked each other questions, and he told me that he was a student for life. Even in his nineties, my grandfather took close-up photos of birds, bees, plants, people, and anything that delighted him. He taught me that curiosity is unending, and that all the questions we ask, whether explainable or not, are miraculous all the same. Most of the time, in our slurry of queries, we realized that neither of us knew the answers, and that was wonderful too. All we knew was that we never wanted to stop asking them. He reminded me that we are always surrounded by beauty, and I am grateful that we could share it with each other. In our shared lifetimes, we were miracle-ing as one.

Perhaps there are some things we were never meant to know. There has been so much deliberation on God and religion that has erupted into violence. We have become hesitant to discuss religion because we are ashamed of our faith or lack thereof. We fear the clash of incompatible opinions. Some of us believe in one God; some of us believe in many gods; some of us believe in the huge and wondrous universe. While atheists might reject the belief of any great creators or deities, not believing is also a belief. Agnostics believe that nothing can be truly known, which is, again, a belief. However, instead of focusing on the differences between our religious beliefs, I wish to explore the core belief that threads us all together: we believe in the mystery of life.

There is a faith that humans hold on to because there is so much that *feels* unexplainable. I say *feel* because while there might be scientific explanations, they still do not convey the reasons *why* we experience life or feel everything in such visceral emotional ways. When people speak of God, I think they are talking about an abstract and mutable truth. We search for meaning because we are so mystified by the illogical sensations that arise when we are moved by the sight of a sunset, the first flecks of a snowfall, or the birth of a child. I think that we are all here for profound reasons, though I do not think we are meant to know them.

Across time and history, religion has often been used by human beings as a tool to harness prejudice, manipulation, and control. Violence and colonial oppression have been used to force people to practice religions, and dissonance in beliefs has led to bloodshed and killings. Some religions have instilled firm binaries of good/evil and heaven/hell and have been used as excuses to create hierarchies and enact genocide, racism, and war. We must learn to discern those as inventions of human ego. When people use religion as an excuse to be violent, they wish to replicate what they perceive to be power. They think that God is control and authority. But I believe that, above anything else, God is an honoring of all life. The tighter we latch on to egotistical forms of "playing God," the further we move from our inner holiness.

Some people turn to religion in times of crisis and trauma because they want to believe in hope beyond devastation. As a queer survivor who was raised Buddhist but went to Catholic school, I experimented with religion after the assault. I prayed to many different deities, read many religious writings, went to churches, temples, and chapels, and found specks of guidance in all of them. While I still feel uncomfortable around some organized forms of religion, mostly because some religious spaces are still queerphobic and transphobic, the most beautiful thing that I witnessed was being in groups of people who were praying deeply for love and healing that was not at the expense of others. There is a strong sense of connection between people in holy spaces, and an ephemeral sense of miracle is ignited when we sing or chant in unison. I believe that any time people come together to celebrate love is a religious experience. It feels grand and almost eerie. The words that come to mind are "larger than life," though I hesitate to use that phrase because life itself is huge and ever expanding.

So maybe the question is not about why we exist, or who exactly God is, but what brings us closer to feeling miraculous. Do you recall those ephemeral and profound moments? What in your body excites you and fills you with comfort and delight? I am called to remember Octavia Butler's groundbreaking quote from *Parable of the Sower*:

> All that you touch
> You Change.
> All that you Change

Changes you.
The only lasting truth
Is Change.
God is change.

Butler is saying that God is the signifier of all life. All beings have the capacity to change, shape-shift, and transform. God
is found in the most intimate moments: in the emotions that overwhelm me when I cry in response to a beautiful song, the unfurling of a new leaf, or the morphing colors of the sky. God is
always embodied, especially when we allow our spirits to speak
through us, when we sing, dance, fall in love, and create beautiful
things. My Buddhism is rooted in my belief that God is everywhere, that God takes every form in the universe, including you
and me. God is when I breathe, when you wake, and when we fall
into deep slumber. God is found in our capacity to love one another. When I remember this, I am moved by my existence, and
yours.

My survival is a miracle. It is miraculous that I survived the abusive
relationship with X. Miracle comes to me when I receive the dawning clarity that I did not deserve the pain that I endured. It comes
when I see myself as whole and sacred before, during, and after the
harm. Each painful moment reveals to me the holiness of my every

breath. No matter how jagged and painful they were, every inhale and exhale was a form of miracle making. It is a miracle that I am still alive, and that I still get to experience love every day.

In our trying times, so many of us are treated as if we were disposable. Rather than being told we are part of an inseparable community of sacred beings, we are told that we are merely parts of a machine. When our functionality determines our worth, we fail to see ourselves as whole in ourselves, whole with one another. When we do not see ourselves as whole, we expect and wait for miracles to come and complete us. We do not believe that they exist within us, and we forget that our existence is a profound miracle too. As our curiosity dims and our wows become quieter, it is easy to forget the miracle of our arrival into this world, especially when we experience hardship, when we struggle, and when we are treated as if we were expendable. However, mindful breathing is a powerful act of remembrance. Each breath I take pulls me back to the miracle of my existence and beckons me to recall how my first breath as a newborn connects to the breath that I take in this very moment. Each breath is sacred because it exists.

When we wait to be completed by external validation, accolades, and achievements, we are hoping to *become* embodiments of perfection. On the contrary, in the Buddhist teachings of Thich Nhat Hanh,* we are taught that we are *born* perfect. Initially, I found this truth confusing. I wondered if that meant that I was

---

*Thich Nhat Hanh passed away while I was completing the final edits of this book. I am deeply grateful for his transcendent existence. This book would not exist without him. All of his work is spectacular, though I learned of this specific wisdom from *The Heart of the Buddha's Teachings*, which is a wonderful introductory text to Buddhism.

perfect no matter what I did, and that I did not have to hold myself accountable for the harm I have caused or the mistakes I have made. I do not think this is the case, because believing that you are born whole does not mean that you are immune to flaws, trauma, and insecurities. All of us are shaped by our experiences, biases, hardships, privileges, and identities, and we adopt many growing pains. What it means is that your being, your aliveness, is perfect, simply because you are here.

When you are present with the now, you are in touch with the perfect truth of your existence, not just in association with the possessions or achievements that inhabit your life. The perfection in your being is not an indication that you have never made a mistake or live a flawless life; instead, it is the wholesome truth that you exist at all. You have a consciousness that beckons you to love yourself enough to hold yourself accountable. You have a consciousness that asks you to love others as you would yourself. When you believe in the perfection of your being, you are in touch with life itself as a core and simple blessing. Sometimes Buddhist philosophies can seem simple, but it is usually the simplicities of our existence that we tend to forget. I believe in honoring the simple miracles.

I used to think that healing was a form of "fixing," and that upon being "healed," I would return to an unharmed version of myself. To find this unharmed version of myself, I would have to trace back to a time impossible to recall. Healing is not the pursuit of purity or pretense, and it is not a journey toward a flawless paradise. In *When Things Fall Apart*, Buddhist nun Pema Chödrön writes of life as being "the path." We may have our eyes set on a destination, a "healed" state, or a place where we can return to ideas of normalcy. However, Chödrön suggests that there is no destination, and that the path is "like riding in a train sitting backwards. We can't see where we're headed, only where we've been." As we look back and reencounter old wounds and painful triggers, we can believe that it will get less difficult, but we cannot expect that all our pain will magically disappear for good. Instead, we must trust that our healing is inherently worthy, abundant, and miraculous, and that "the source of wisdom is whatever is happening to us right at this very instant." Healing is a perpetual form of change and adaptation, and an act of compassion that we learn to extend toward ourselves. Healing is not clutching at ideas of who we were before we were harmed but remembering that we were always born whole. Healing teaches us that we are forever deserving of love.

The path has been treacherous, and it has also been full of love. Both of those truths merge into a bittersweet combination. When I learned to be in loving relationship with myself, I had to open my heart to the possibilities of falling in love again. I had to fall in love with the world around and within me. Falling in love can feel like a magical and godly event, though it also makes us feel vulnerable and brings us closer to our truths, whether we are ready to face them or not. When X and I fell in love, we spent far more time obsessing over the miracle of our union than the miracles that we both contained in ourselves. It has taken me a long time to realize that healing is not a path that leads to a heavenly destination. Instead, it's a path that brings me back to my own wholeness. And it is a path that never ends—it extends into an ongoing journey of gratitude, nurturance, and curiosity. Being in relationship is the coming together of miracles and being in love is imagining what it means to miracle together, as a holy and ever-continuing act.

A few years after the assault, I returned to California. I spent six months there, and I had enough courage to revisit some of the places that X and I explored together. I thought of him every now and then, though those places were no longer dominated by memories of our relationship. I explored the mountains, the ocean, the forests, and even went to a natural hot spring that was named after miracles. When it was time to return to New York, I decided to take the train by myself across the country. I had always wanted to do this, and I fantasized about sitting in solitude and watching the landscape change and pass me by. The cross-country train ride was sixty-six hours long, and I would travel through Arizona, New Mexico, Colorado, Kansas, and Missouri, across the expansiveness of the land. I embarked on the journey alone.

On the first day, I made friends with the people in my carriage. Most of my new friends were in their sixties and seventies, and we quickly bonded over our mutual excitement for the journey to come. There were four of us, and we swiftly became a tight-knit group capable of endless conversation. Each of us told our stories, intentions, dreams, passions, and the reasons why we were traveling the country by train. We all had different destinations, though we shared the same desire to see Earth in all her grandeur from the comforts of a moving train. Going on a cross-country road trip was part of our dreams, and we were all meeting one another in the miracle. It did not take long for us to make plans, and so we arranged to have dinner together in the dining car at sunset.

The dinner we shared was filled with lively conversation, and we all exchanged personal, strange, and interesting stories of our lives. It was easy to be open because I was surrounded by such invigorated and curious people. We all lived vastly different lives that varied in privilege, race, class, and location and had many experiences in different countries, historical moments, and sociopolitical environments. We explored a wide range of topics, and it almost seemed as if we could not run out of things to talk about until we arrived at the topic of God. Initially, talking about God was uncomfortable, because there was a hesitance to expose our inevitable differences in beliefs. However, after a few minutes, we dove in, and we spoke about our beliefs candidly. I explained that I did not believe there was one almighty figure of God, but that God, Buddha, the universe, or whatever we chose to call it, was in everything, including us. I shared that I saw God in small intimate moments: the crawling of vines, a bird's song, and the crystal clarity of water. Even though they did not all agree, everyone listened with thoughtfulness and intent. I then asked everybody the question "When have you seen or experienced God?" and funnily enough, we all pointed to the sunset. We showed one another pictures of sunsets we had witnessed in our lives, the rosy and pastel hues that left us staring in awe, and then looked outside at the fiery orb that was setting over the majestic canyons.

One of the people in our group, an Ethiopian man on his way to see the Grand Canyon by himself, shared a deeply moving anecdote with us. I am immensely grateful that he has granted me permission to recount it in this chapter. He began his story by telling us about his childhood. He had not experienced much affection as a child and had gone through a lot of hardship back home. He had not heard the words "I love you" while growing up. When he was older, he decided to move to America in hopes of a fresh start to embark on his career and experience the grand promises that America had to offer. He was hopeful and excited, and when he arrived, he used all his precious savings to buy himself a new car.

Unfortunately, soon after acquiring the car, he had an accident and the car was totaled. He survived the crash, but it left him in a dire financial position. In that moment, even though it seemed like a point of utter despair, he was viscerally aware of his aliveness and his survival, and the sky above him began to open. As he looked around him, he heard, reverberating in the clear and vast world above, a clear and crisp "I love you." He said that this was his first time hearing those precious words, and that they hit him like a bolt of lightning. He knew that it was the voice of God. He felt so lucky and grateful because in that moment, he saw that his life was holy and that love was all around him. He told this story with a huge grin on his face, bursting at the seams with love.

We all grew quiet, touched by his story, and paused our lively conversation. We all drifted away into thought, and I knew we were all immersed in a miracle. Golden sunbeams poured into the windows as they reflected off the maroon desert canyons passing by us. I peered into the sunset, as it connected to my miracle and the miracle of every person at the table. Tears rolled down my face, and I was grateful that we were there, miracle-ing together.

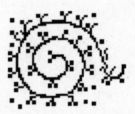

TEN

LOVE

Unconditional Love Is Embodied

I like to gaze at the sky whenever I can. It is a practice that I try to commit to as frequently as possible. Whenever I find the time, even if I am on the bus or waiting for time to pass, I try to remind myself to observe the world above. I often forget about the perspective that the vast abyss has to offer, and sometimes I am shocked by the stark shades of blue and the billowing, floating clouds. I am looking up at the sky now, as I write to you. A calm breeze caresses my cheek. Perhaps if you looked toward the sky right now, you, too, would be surprised. As you look up, take a deep breath in. Know that I am here with you, in this very precious moment. Where I am, the breeze is soft and generous, and it is creating a gentle applause with the looming trees. The trees are with us, too, and they are whispering to us that they are proud of us, not just for our achievements, but for our wondrous survival. The clouds drift above, some of them wispy and some of them thick, bouncy, and dense. They remind me that nothing is ever still and that we are in perpetual movement. Just like the desert, the sky appears to be an expansive chasm of possibilities. We cannot control or capture the air around us, so let us honor its many shapes as it holds us in its infinity.

As I stare at the cloud formations, I realize that nothing ever stays the same. Sometimes I feel inclined to capture the clouds in their shapes. I want to bottle up the cloud formations that I feel so moved by. I see scorpions and dragons and hearts in the sky, and I want to make them mine. I must breathe deeply and notice the intent behind that desire. It comes from a struggle to adapt to change as it comes, and it originates from a place of thinking that I must possess what gives me pleasure. Everything around me that is alive, or that is made of something that once was alive, is an agent of change. To love each of these beings with wholeness is to see them fully as they come, go, connect with me, and pass me by. As I look to the same sky during each shifting season, I notice new moments and gifts in love. I see new symbols in the sky, dewdrops forming with the morning air, fluffy white snow falling from the abundant abyss, and birds soaring home. As I have learned from the meditations of Thich Nhat Hanh,* I take a deep breath in—I have arrived. I take a deep breath out—I am home.

In recent years, even breath has become something to regard warily, with distrust. We wear masks to protect ourselves and others from a virus that travels through the air. I am saddened by this

---

*I learned these meditations from his teachings of mindfulness at Plum Village.

development, though I must remind myself that it is not the air that we fear, but the virus that travels through it. We are trying our best to liberate one another from the confines of the virus and keep everyone safe. We are striving to make sure that when we gather, we do so responsibly, in consideration of the people with whom we may not personally have relationships but care for all the same.

Similarly, love surrounds us as a powerful force that we often tend to distrust. So many sensations travel through love, and all our projections, traumas, and pain create contortions of confusion, fear, and hardship. We must remember that it is not love that we are afraid of. We fear the abandonment, betrayal, violence, and abuse that come with the complexities of human trauma and relationships. We cannot fear love because love is embodied. Just as air only becomes breath when it is held within our strong expansive lungs, love only comes into existence through us. If we fear love, then what we truly fear is ourselves. We can never be separated from love.

Love is as essential as the air that we breathe. It is all around us, always enveloping us in its swirling embrace. It is an essential part of our being, and it is magical because it takes many different shapes. It allows us to experience joy, laughter, connectivity, aliveness, and has existed long before the lineages of our ancestors. Despite love's enduring and eternal presence, we, as a human species, still cannot seem to dissect, define, or even truly understand it. We all have our own interpretations of it, colored by our experiences and warped by our fears. Instead of trying to understand love, perhaps we could reconnect with *being* it. We always seem to be searching for love, and yet tend to forget that love has a home in us.

Perhaps love confuses us because it comes without definition. It is as expansive and perplexing as the infinity of the sky. In a world that is defined by binaries, a force as unexplainable as love can be confusing and mysterious. Maybe love does not wish to be understood but yearns to be felt and remembered. As Linda Hogan writes poetically in *Dwellings*, "At times, when we are silent enough, still enough, we take a step into such mystery, the place of spirit, and mystery, we must remember, by its very nature does not wish to be known." Love is mysterious, unexplainable, indefinable. As mutable as air, it holds millions of simultaneous truths.

During our lifetimes, we will experience love with dawning clarity. Moments in love will appear to us in sudden bursts of light, interlacing themselves elegantly in the relationships that we nurture, and in beautiful, random, serendipitous experiences. Love, like the grand sky, cannot be captured by us and locked in a cage. Love is constant and is the force that keeps us alive. Love is as mutable, undefinable, divine, and essential as the great atmospheric beyond. Love is not obtained; love is embodied. Love is freeing, and loving is free.

X always told me that I did not love him unconditionally. He said that unconditional love meant that we loved each other no matter what, even when he acted violently toward me. I was familiar with this sentiment, as I had grown up in a family with the same ideas.

We would fight and harm one another, and instead of engaging in conflict resolution or committing to nonviolence in our household, we would brush off our harm by saying, "This is what families do. We fight, but we stick together and love one another no matter what." While I understand the intention behind those ideas of enduring love, I also think that it can be unloving to make excuses for our harmful behavior. When such excuses are made, nothing changes, and the harm only festers and continues. Similarly, X's ideas of unconditional love meant that he would always be provided with unconditional allowance to continue his harmful behaviors. He manipulated me into thinking that I was the problem whenever I wanted to leave. Instead of holding himself accountable for his harmful actions, he told me that I was not loving enough.

The definition of "unconditional love" cannot be clear until we reflect on the definition of love itself. Since the dawn of time, love has slipped away from the confines of being definable. However, I am ever grateful for those who have articulated their visions of love through poetry, song, and art, and I believe that everybody's definition has a morsel of love's ever-growing wisdom. In *All about Love*, bell hooks writes about what practicing true love requires of us.

> To begin by always thinking of love as an action rather than a feeling is one way in which anyone using the word in this manner automatically assumes accountability and responsibility. We are often taught we have no control over our "feelings." Yet most of us accept that we choose our actions, that intention and will inform what we do. We also accept that our actions have consequences.

She concludes the paragraph by explaining the six ingredients of love:

When we are loving we openly and honestly express care, affection, responsibility, respect, commitment, and trust.

Love is embedded with choice—that's what bell hooks teaches us. All our relationships are different, and we are the inventors, imaginers, and creators of what mutual affection, respect, commitment, and trust can be. When we commit to being in loving relationships, whether with lovers, family, friends, or Earth, we have a responsibility to nurture those six crucial ingredients. While X may have had strong feelings for me, his actions toward me were far from loving. His need to violate and control me did not honor the responsibilities he assumed as my partner. Love cannot be captured, controlled, or obtained, and loving relationships require intentional choices that will allow all parties to feel free from our preconceived notions of power and possession. X defended his behaviors by hiding behind his "passionate" feelings for me, making excuses that he loved me too much and could not control himself. Be that as it may, he could have made many choices to treat me, and himself, differently. In the end, the most loving thing that he did for me was leave. Sometimes our relationships are so difficult that separating can be an act of love. Love as a feeling is simply not enough.

Love is not just felt sporadically. It is a continuous act that energizes our every move. When we acknowledge that love is threaded into every choice that we make, we can see ourselves as sources of love. Love not only ebbs and flows around us but also resides in our spirits. While there are many things that we cannot control, in our relationships we should have agency over what we choose to commit to. The healthiest loving choices require us to unlearn the violent ideas of romance we have been conditioned to crave. When we choose to be in relationship with another person, we are choosing to connect our sacred sources of love. Contrary to X's beliefs, loving each other unconditionally is not staying for the sake of preserving a feeling, but choosing to act toward each other in ways that are kind, respectful, affectionate, and without the need for domination, ownership, and control. Thanks to the wisdoms of bell hooks, I have learned that honoring our relationships is committing to love as a constant and lively action.

So many of us have been taught to morph into idealized versions of ourselves to obtain our lovers' affections. I have concealed my flaws and flattened my complexities to act as the perfect love interest. When I was with X, I often accentuated my femininity, although I kept it measured because I knew that it also threatened him. Setting those unrealistic expectations erased layers of my multidimensional mutable personhood. When we perform for our partners, we are still existing under a set of mythical conditions that have been ingrained in us. It is painful and dishonest to confine ourselves to societal standards of desirability. If we must enact these charades to please our partners, then we are only being desired as figments and fantasies. We are not free in those relationships, but still restricted to a set of limiting rules.

It requires ample vulnerability to arrive at true closeness. We must see one another fully and offer love and support when we arrive at our struggles. Unconditional love is seeing one another, and ourselves, wholly and with compassion. It is where we can be curious and compassionate about all our similarities and differences.

We will be challenged to be wholly honest with others and move through the fear of our own murky truths. To be loving is to find new ways to protect one another, unearth the roots of our intergenerational trauma, and honor our responsibilities as lovers in the world. It requires us to see other people as whole beings with agency, complexities, and miraculous aliveness, while also acknowledging that we are delicately intertwined.

X and I wanted to be the only sources of each other's joy, and we were both threatened when we felt as if we could not provide something to each other. We strove to be each other's everything and narrowed each other's worlds. We did our relationship a huge disservice by living in such spiritual scarcity. And how exhausting it was to maintain the role of being the sole source of each other's glee! In *Airman's Odyssey*, Antoine de Saint-Exupéry wrote, "Love does not consist in gazing at each other but in looking outward together in the same direction." It is when we have accepted that we can no longer be the sole source of each other's bliss that we can encourage ourselves and others to seek exuberance at its fullest and brightest. It is an honor when we can meet each other in celebration at junctures of our jubilation and meet with tenderness at the crossroads of our grief. Being in loving relationship is sharing the abundance that life has to offer, for there is so much to love. It comes without the condition of being physically close, or even in a committed relationship. It is when we can think of the people we love and feel uplifted when we envision their healing and their happiness. Unconditional love comes without trying to be each other's "everything" but feeling grateful that we exist in this vast everything together.

Who are our teachers in unconditional love? In *True Love*, Thich Nhat Hanh presents a beautiful meditation that I practice all the time. The first mantra is "Dear one, I am here for you." Then you take a deep breath. The second mantra is "Dear one, I know that you are here, and it makes me very happy." Then you take another deep intentional breath. I look toward our wise mother Earth and speak these mantras to her, and I hear her saying them back to me. As I sit under the crown of a family of trees, they tell me that they are happy that I am here. I see the trees swaying in the breeze, so wise in their existence, providing me shade and breath and loving me for my existence. When the sun kisses my body, I feel loved just for being alive. Our aliveness intertwines, and I absorb the energy that the sun so generously and unconditionally provides. I am being loved as I deserve to be loved, and I learn from that love how to share it with you. Loving each other for the simplicity of our being is a beautiful place to start. Thich Nhat Hanh writes, "If you practice in this way, with a lot of concentration and mindfulness, you will see that this person will open immediately, like a flower blossoming. To be loved is to be recognized, and you can do that several times a day. It is not difficult at all, and it is a true meditation." As we try our best to see and love our partners, family, and friends with fullness, we can always return to gratitude as our first loving choice.

One of our most sacred relationships is with ourselves. As we commit to the close relationships in our lives, we need to make sure that we are always simultaneously pouring love into our very own beings. Because we are getting to know ourselves as sources of love, we might become very good at providing love, while forgetting how it feels to receive. My therapist once told me that receiving love is just as important as giving it, and that I needed to honor my role as both provider and recipient. I need to engage in a reciprocal exchange of love where I no longer erase myself from the equation. It was profound when I used bell hooks's six ingredients of love as a guideline to ask myself: Do I show care and respect toward myself? Do I trust myself, and do I commit to treating myself with kindness and affection? Asking myself these questions was already an act of love, and I could feel my heart expanding as I began to receive.

I misunderstood self-love when it became popularized. I had a very basic understanding of it and thought that it meant to be selfish and hyper-individualistic. In my heartbreak, I thought that self-love meant to hoard all my love for myself. I became my top priority, and everything else came after. If something did not "serve" me, I quickly cut it out. I started treating people as if they were disposable, especially during conflict. Now, in hindsight, it feels violent to me to think of anything in the world as living to serve. I started meeting a lot of other people who engaged in the same form of narcissism that they thought was self-love. However, I noticed that when we all spoke of "self-love," we all spoke with protective emotional shields. Because my trust had been betrayed, I told myself that "the only person I can trust is myself" and built walls blocking me from possibilities of intimacy and communion. Dedicating my love to hyper-individualism did not nourish love, and instead severed my ties to all the love I was connected to. Loving myself did not mean that I had to confine myself to an island and loving my life did not mean that I had to venture through it alone. I had forgotten that my pleasure is connected to all pleasure, my sorrow is connected to all sorrow, and my joy is connected to all joy. Self-love is not narcissistic selfishness, nor is it isolation. Self-love connects us to all the loving forces that surround us. Self-love dissolves the barriers between us and others. When we deeply love ourselves, we love one another.

Loving myself with fullness means thinking of my emotional responses and coping mechanisms as acts of love that are being communicated through my body. They all guide me toward a clarifying awareness of the choices that I need to make to honor myself and my loved ones. Listening to myself, identifying my survival mechanisms, seeing where my actions are coming from, and being patient with myself are all acts of self-love. Being compassionate with myself when I have caused or experienced harm allows me to get to the root of my behaviors. It allows me to no longer treat myself as an enemy but as a vulnerable person who requires care. Self-love is not about building yourself up to become a perfect, "lovable" person, but realizing that you are worthy of love simply because you are here.

I cannot demand that somebody love themselves as if it were an easy or graceful task. Most of us—especially if we come from marginalized groups—were not taught to love ourselves from a young age. We were taught to aspire toward a hierarchized white, straight, male, cisgender, able-bodied, and wealthy supremacy, while dedicating our lives to being in servitude to it. Self-hatred is allocated and manufactured, and corporations both instill and profit from the self-doubt of millions of people. Now, these very same corporations are profiting from trendy portrayals of self-love and marketing it as a tool for consumption. These corporations endeavor to turn self-love into consumerist products, when self-love is the opposite of the palatable. Self-love is a grueling task of getting to know yourself with deep compassion. It requires us to swim in our shadows, laugh at our quirks, and unlearn, with compassion, all the conditions that have pushed us far away from unconditional love. Self-love is nourished and embodied, not attained.

In high school, I looked up to the popular white girls. They ostracized me, made fun of my family, and laughed at the working-class neighborhood I lived in. I believed that I was as disposable and interchangeable as they said I was. My insecurities grew, as I was taught to crave white supremacy, yearn for an impossible reality, and construct a mask to conceal my culture and depths. I thought that they treated me like that because they loved themselves and their whiteness so much, though now in hindsight I know that they were clutching at their whiteness with fear. Their "confidence" was not a love that they had nurtured for their being; instead, it was so fragile that they required the suffering of non-white people to feel good. That is not self-love. While white spiritual practitioners and corporations might find it easy to ask somebody to love themselves, it is imperative that they start by considering who exactly has the privilege of growing up encouraged to love themselves in the first place. Self-love is nonhierarchical and is not compatible with superiority complexes. As I fall in love with myself, I am accessing the vast wells of love that have existed within me long before I was conditioned to forget about them.

I thought that my first love was X, when really my first love existed way before I was born. In *The Teachings on Love*, Thich Nhat
Hanh wrote, "You will discover your 'first love' was not really the
first. Many streams nourish and support the river of your life. Your
first love has no beginning and no end; it is always in transformation. Your first love is still present, continuing to shape your life."
When I think of my first love as an ever-growing and shape-
shifting force, I feel liberated from my attachments to X. Assign-
ing X the role of my first love put a lot of pressure on our
relationship. The more I strained to preserve our attachment, the
harder it was to let go. One of the reasons I repeatedly returned to
him was because I was attached to the significance and romantici-
zation of our relationship. I believed that my first love would also
be my last. It has been liberating to see that love did not begin or
end with X; love always had a home in me. Even if our first loving
relationships are healthy, they are still not our first loves. Our love
follows a lineage of moving time and existence, unbound by history and flowing from the universe. Instead of seeking our "first
loves" in our relationships, perhaps we should get to know the unending love that oscillates from within.

My love for myself is a sacred connection that extends and
stretches into an interdependent love. Contrary to what I believed,
the love that I poured into myself did not deplete a finite supply of
love. The more I poured into myself, the more it multiplied in
abundance. I took myself on romantic dates, gave myself permission to go to therapy, asked my loved ones for reciprocal care,
communicated openly and honestly, admitted hard truths, read
books in the sun, and shared unconditional love with Earth. Being
gentle with myself, reparenting myself, and romancing myself

strengthened all my relationships. Loving myself required neither exclusivity nor supremacy; it built a sacred bridge that brought me closer to my first love that existed long before me.

Two years after the assault, I discovered that X had moved to another country. We had not spoken since the day that he left me. I was in New York, and we were very far apart. Upon learning about his move, I was shocked into slow motion. I had been submerged in such deep grief, and the news of his move reminded me that he was still somewhere out there. He was alive. Even though our geographic distance meant that I would be physically safe from his harm, I was not ecstatic about it. My anxiety spiked, and it was as if I were starting a new grieving cycle. He was really gone. It was truly over. My body still craved the rhythm of our chaos, although now I was aware that I was longing for an unhealthy delusion of love. My healing process had been immensely challenging, though the generosity of time allowed my soma to slowly acclimate to his absence. He started to morph into a fuzzy dream, and with each passing day I was able to see with inklings of clarity how much I had romanticized the symbolic relevance of our relationship: I did not miss him as a person; I missed him as the figure of my first romantic love.

The new rhythms of my everyday life bored me at first. Even though I was immersed in the lively spirit of New York City, the chaos did not compare to the disarray of my relationship with X.

In contrast, it felt almost dull. I was no longer receiving fifty phone calls a day demanding to know my whereabouts, accusing me of being promiscuous, and insulting me with slurs. I sought chaos by going to parties, though I was surprised by how wholesome some of these spaces were, especially those made for and by queer and trans people of color.* People really looked out for one another and made sure that we were all feeling safe and free. I saw love in action, even in the organized chaos. I started to nurture the friendships I had made at parties and ventured outside the club. The relationships I was forming showed me radical forms of care, and I did not feel constricted or surveilled. Amid everything that we were fighting and resisting, my friends taught me how to feel free in the fullness of my being. New rhythms were emerging for me, and my soma was both pleased and confused.

The night I found out that X had moved away, I uncharacteristically decided to stay home. I sat alone in my dimly lit room, acutely aware of the commotion of the city rushing past me. I felt grounded and ready for something despite not knowing what it was. As I listened to the sirens and the scurrying sleeplessness of the city, I burst into tears. I was crying because I felt so moved and alive. I could viscerally feel the reemergence of the agency I thought I had lost long ago, and I was making new and loving choices for myself. Moving to the city was one of the first choices I made that was not bound to pleasing X. Here I was, sitting in a room of my own, and I was profoundly proud of myself. I wept out of both exhaustion and elation and repeatedly said to myself,

---

*Shout-out to so many of my friends who are nightlife organizers. You all changed my life.

212 • Be Not Afraid of Love

"This has been so fucking hard, but I feel so free." I said this five times, almost like a mantra. I stared out my window and opened my computer because I wanted to write my sentimental feelings down. I checked my email, and amid my unorganized in-box, I saw it: an email from X. It was as if he could sense that I was feeling good. Another one of life's unnerving mysteries was that somehow he always returned when he could sense my strength. It was as if the universe were testing me. I trembled as I clicked on it. It read:

> I'll keep it short but, I just wanna say, from all of me, that I'm sorry for how everything turned out. I love you and I hope you're doing alright. I look forward to the day when we're together again.

I observed my reaction. I was solemn, scared, and disgusted. Something significant inside me had shifted. As I read the message repeatedly, my fury grew like an expanding mass of hot air. I could see on the screen that the words "I love you" held no romance, no thought, and no care. It was clear to me that he had reached out to make a statement, to first overwhelm me with emotion, and to alleviate his own guilt by giving me a brief apology without any accountability. His last sentiment was particularly audacious and revealed to me his true intentions. He wanted to find a way back into my life, and as far as he was concerned, I had no agency: the matter was out of my control; I had no choice. In his world, if he decided that he wanted us to get back together, then it was solely his decision to make. I was no more than a lifeless doll, easily contorted and willfully handled as he pleased. Upon looking back, nothing had changed, and his narcissistic apology revealed that to him, I was nothing more than a vessel that he could use and discard at his whim.

Over the next few weeks, I reread this declarative "I love you" many times over. After the hundredth time, a crystalline clarity formed before me: He did not love me. That was not love. He did not have the capacity to nurture, foster, or heal a meaningful relationship with me, and he did not have a loving relationship with himself. What I had believed so long to be love was not love, and it was liberating to finally see that dawning truth. As I observed my reactions, I felt close to myself. I knew that I was still getting to know myself, and that I was so much more than he could ever imagine.

The meaning of love struck me like a divine intervention. X's words were now rendered meaningless to me because I could tell that he was saying them to get what he wanted. I felt so loved in this moment, not by him but by myself. His unloving actions brought me closer to my source of love because I could finally see that he was showing me the opposite of it. He did not care about my freedom, well-being, or agency. In his eyes I was nothing but a figment of a dream. The silk screen of our romance had been punctured and destroyed. As I saw through the lies that he was telling, both to me and to himself, my agency was activated. Upon the realization that he did not care about my freedom, he inadvertently set me free from his emotional control. These displays of "passion" felt familiar to me, but I did not want them anymore. I felt myself opening; my fear of true love was starting to dissolve. That was a milestone in my healing. I was unclouded about what I wanted and what I deserved. I had come such a long way. It was so fucking hard, but I felt so fucking free.

There are moments in love that we experience with lucidity. We cannot explain it, but we just know that what we are experiencing is a deep and true moment in love, even if it is shared with a stranger. It is deeply instinctual, and often unexplainable. I think about strolling through the tree-lined streets of Brooklyn, witnessing lovers dancing to a Louis Armstrong song playing in the distance. I remember my sacred guardian, the hummingbird, that hovered outside my window for weeks. I recall reading Robin Wall Kimmerer's *Braiding Sweetgrass* alone in bed and weeping while I learned about the kinship of plants. I think of the estuary, a meeting place of many spirits, and the ocean, a place where I finally learned to let go. I fondly reminisce about dancing in parks, meditating with the Vietnamese monks in the monastery, and teaching virtual writing workshops with young and eager writers who all burst into tears by the end of the class. I remember learning how to celebrate and forgive myself with compassion. I remember every sunset, and I remember wanting to live.

When we experience these moments in love, it feels like the spirits of our first loves returning to us. Moments like these spur a blossoming within me and allow me to open to new possibilities of love: I witness an older gentleman taking a nap in the sun, the first flowers blooming into life during the spring, and my two-year-old neighbor leaving a little orange blossom for me on my stoop. I picture my friends caressing my hands and feet after the assault, my mother making dumplings for me and my family, and my queer friends sharing nights under many full moons. As I feel my heart opening, I see that the universe is always conspiring to bring us closer together. I am no longer afraid of closeness because every breath I take is a chance to feel close to the world.

I watched a film called *After Life* by Hirokazu Kore-eda, which is a fictional story of twenty Japanese people who had just passed away. Before their spirits were released into the spirit world, they had to pass through a facility that offered them a unique service. The service required every person to recount their most treasured memory so that those memories could be re-created on film. Upon watching that film, the deceased people would take that memory to the spirit realm, where it would happily play on an infinite loop. To my surprise, every single person who recounted their cherished memories shared extremely simple moments. A man talked about how he felt as a little boy when a soft breeze blew through the windows of his school bus. Another man recalled how happy he was when he talked to his wife on a park bench. And an older woman recalled the beauty of watching cherry blossom petals drifting down like snow during the springtime. All these memories were so simple, but so full of love. They were reminders of life, mystery, and the poetic rhythms of change.

I think about my late grandfather and how he introduced me to classical music for the first time. He showed me that my emotions held ample validity, and that I was worthy of love even if I was imperfect. He watched my birth and always treated my life like a miracle. Every time I hear the flourishing of piano keys or the dramatic serenade of strings, I think of my grandfather and how my birth is connected to his existence and his passing. He is still everywhere around me; he is in birdsong, the full moon, and the delicate wings of a butterfly. He is right here with me, for love does not vanish, and death is not the end.

What are your moments in love?

Now, I am on a flight back to Australia after four years away. I am soaring through the sky and there are thick fluffy masses of clouds below me. They are traveling in packs, moving slowly and densely through the vast ether. As I travel through this expansive un-known, I realize that I am flying through the very sky that I have so often feared. I am submerged in blue and I feel closer than ever to the sun's warmth. I am reminded that the sun is always shining brightly as Earth continues to turn, even when we cannot see it. All around me, I see the constancy of change. On this plane I am reflecting on the past few years as I return to my place of origin. I am going back to the place I was born, and I am returning whole, taking home with me the strength and guidance of my chosen family and everybody who has shown me care. I will reunite once more with new dimensions, emerging wounds, and finally be able to honor my beloved grandfather's ashes.

A nostalgic feeling clings to the open air. There is a swelling in my chest, and I am filled with sentimentality. I am thinking about how I moved to Turtle Island on my own and found a community of miraculous queers. I am reminiscing about my experiences with

my grandfather and thinking about how committed I am to healing my relationships with my biological family. In this short burst
of miraculous time we share, I am determined to nurture all our
sacred interconnections. X pops into my mind, and I realize that
the more I have gotten to know myself, the more he feels like a
stranger. There have been so many departures and transitions, and
as I enter another one, there is a twinkle in the air that offers me
the promise of falling in love. I look to the heavens and realize that
I am already deeply in love with my aliveness.

Since X, I have not yet fallen in romantic love again. I do not
seek romance as a desperate distraction like I used to, though my
heart is wide open to the arrival of romantic love as a blessing in my
life. I have experienced love in so many forms, and I do not depend
on romance to embody love, though I wish to welcome its abundant poetry all the same. It has taken ample time and patience, but
I am excited and equipped with a tender sense of awareness.

When I say be not afraid of love, I do not mean that we should
rid ourselves of fear, but that we should sit with our fear and learn
to love it too. I love my entire embodied being. Instead of pointing
a trembling finger at love, I look closely and gently at my fear. I
allow myself the fullness of my feelings and I do not push myself
away when difficult emotions arise. Love is sitting with the vastness of my numbness, the sacred breath of my rage, the prickliness
of my knowing, the ceremonies of my grief. Love reveals the truth
to us because love is the truth. To be committed to love is to be
committed to the infinite life of change. I know now that I must
not fear love, for I am love. We all are.

Love is the honoring of our interconnected aliveness, and I am
so grateful that I have survived.

Acknowledgments

Gratitude is a muscle that I constantly wish to exercise, so I am excited that I can write pages dedicated to the people, places, and poetry that I am grateful for.

I am grateful for my mother, Betty Wong, with whom my relationship has blossomed and grown so much. Thank you for being supportive of my long writing journey, and for using your brilliant intuition to trust in mine. Distance has truly made our hearts grow both fonder and closer, and you were the first person on this Earth who taught me about unconditional love and care. The miracle of my presence is indebted to yours.

Thank you to my brothers, Edwin and Alvin Zhu. I am so proud of you both for coming closer to your dreams. Edwin, I am so excited to see your world expand and soar. It is an honor to watch you mature with such mindfulness. Alvin, your dedication to your vision manifests into something stronger each day, and you really teach me about putting your heart into everything you do. Thank you both for always being so present in your care.

To my father, Tim Zhu, thank you for sharing your deep passion for education with me. It is because of you that I have grown into such an avid reader and thinker. It is so sweet and comical that now that I am older, I can appreciate the ways that you walk around our garden listening to socialist podcasts all day. It makes so much sense that I, too, have such an active hunger for knowledge. Thank you for always sharing your curiosity with me; it has been such a blessing to see you blossom with the gardens that you tend to.

Thank you to my ye ye (grandfather), Sidney Charles Scott, who passed away in August 2020. I am grateful for your eternal guiding light, for the way that you stayed forever curious and open-minded. You taught me how to ask questions, and that I am a student for life. Thank you for showing me a love so different from the love that society taught me to strive for. I hold that every day, and I know that your spirit lives on forever.

Immense love to my biological families spread across the world on our different paths and experiences of immigration. With love to the Wong families and the Zhu families, who continue to unfold in abundant lineages.

I am deeply grateful for my chosen families in so many places. First, to my chosen kin whom I met in the Bay Area. Without you, I may not have been able to escape and heal from the assault as I did. Thank you for introducing me to queer kinship and showing me support during one of the most difficult times in my life. An especially huge thank-you to Journye Deloney and Sim Wallace for being the most loyal Scorpio friends I could ever hope for.

I also wanted to thank Piper Jackson, Darlene Albert, Rewina Beshue, Audrey Stuart, Eric Torres, Aroma, Hanna Chen, Fayth Yono, Lindsay Rodriguez, Alora King Villa LeMalu, Diana Kim, Sal Tran, Azha Luckman, and Isabella Kim.

I write with love to my best friend and life partner, Sammy Kim, whom I intend to know and love forever. It is because of you that I have been able to stay still and find the space to write while being surrounded by queer tenderness, joy, and celebration. I thank you for showing up for me consistently, and for making our promises of eternal love at sunset on Robbi's rooftop.

Of course, immense love to my chosen family in New York. Without you, I would not be Mimi Zhu. It was there that I felt comfortable and confident enough to truly embody that name. It was there that I really began to cry and find liberation in those tears. It was in New

York that I was encouraged to write, to share, and to publish my words. It is there that I realized the many colorful and nonbinary identities that live within me, and where I could radiate the myriad energies that you all see and hold. It is there that I received a reeducation in relationships and an abundance of celebratory joy. We celebrated being alive every day we could, and I am humbly grateful to the collectives and organizations—Anti-Violence Project, BUFU, Plum Village, Radical Love Consciousness, Papi Juice, Wing On Wo, Aerthship, Discakes, Club Carry, Asian American Writers' Workshop, Yellow Jackets Collective, Playground Coffee Shop, Bubble T, API Rainbow Parents, Young New Yorkers—that taught me information, celebration, intersection, and adoration.

I specifically wish to mention the many names of people who I met in New York who have supported, inspired, and loved me throughout the years: Sammy Kim, Cherry Jaymes, Yusuf Siddiqui, Felah Voltaire, Nuur Salam (you are the reason I experienced the Queer World), LoAn Nguyen, Fariha Roisin, Sonia Prabhu, Neema Githere, Munachi Osegbu, Lawyer Opoku, Coco Layne, Francisco Rodriguez, Shai Jones, Sandy Taboo, Angel aka Ninfa, Exo aka Etoile Bright, Indra Budiman, Eleven Reilly, Mina Le, Citlali Gutierrez, Robbi Sy, Prinita Thevarajah, Gabe Dortala Fontaine, Tsige Tafesse, Katherine Tom, Yeelen Cohen, Luis Corrales, Ayqa Khan, Arslan Mehal, Mohammed Iman, Oscar Nunez, Adam Rhodes, Victoria Foster, Mitchell Kuga, Somnath Bhatt, Betty Mulat, Terrell Villiers, ELSZ, Alexander Chee, Michelle Ling, Esther Hur, Parissah Lin, Vincent Chong, Yerim Choi, Kit Lee, Kit Yan, Steph Lau, Bo Suh, Poppy Liu, Sandy Hong, Yoon Na, Navya Cherukuru, Natalia Mantini, Kay Thebez, Jaylen Strong, Duneska Suanette Michel, Zenat Begum, Rin Kim, Arabelle Sicardi, Zeba Blay, Yrsa Daley-Ward, Alice Sparkly Kat, Thanu Yakupitiyage, Fran Tirado, Olivia McKayla Ross, Mena Sachdev, Saji Gabriel Abude, Niki Franco, Ash Rucker, Izzy Webb, Adam Intrator, Tin Mai, Khoa Sinclair, Crystal Simone, Travis Brown, Kayla Quan, Francesse Dolbrice,

Netty Fremont, Syd Falls, Roby Saludares, Meng Wen Cao, West Dakota, Andrew Nguyen, Dylan Thomas (a.k.a. Mthr Trsa), Henry Bae, Zi, Dare Teng, Justin Wee, Shaobo Han, Louis Dorantes, Nicholas Anderson, Stevie Huynh, Pedro Vidallon, Paul Tran, Karlo Bueno Bello, Clara Lu, Sho Konishi, and, last but not least, Maggie James.

A deep thank-you to my agent, Clare Mao, who asked me so calmly if I wanted to make my dreams come true. You have truly guided me (and many incredible artists whom I have the privilege to know) toward the fruition of my brightest dreams. You have provided me the best experience I could have asked for with my first published book, and I have felt so safe and taken care of in your loving hands. You have made it possible for so many queer Asian artists to create freely and expansively. You are truly a gift.

I found out about my book deal offer while on a drive to Miracle Hot Springs in California. I was in the car with two of my best friends, Fatima Nieto and Munachi Osegbu, and we were passing sprawling mountains and fields of green and blue. You both cried when we heard the update, and I was so moved by the way you held me through this life-changing news. I love you both. I want to thank my dear friends on the West Coast for providing me support while I wrote half of my book out there. Big love to Noah Pham (thank you for allowing me to sleep on your couch during times of heartbreak), Edgar Neri, Justin Cayco, Aaron Lim, Danny Nguyen, Jinro, Jasmine Corrales, Brinda Iyer, Sukhpreet Purewal, Kari Dramé, Gabi Richardson, Coyote Park, Malik D. Flournoy-Hooker, Raveena Aurora, Alex Sia, Leandy Wu, Amy Lee, Loveis Wise, Britt Martinez-Hewitt, Jas Lin, Lupita Corrales, Alexa Demie, Melanie Martinez, and Pony Hurtado.

Eternal thanks to my editors, Victoria Savanh and Amy Sun, two Asian American women who have shown me such kindness and brilliance. Victoria, I remember speaking to you in the initial stages of bookmaking and already feeling an instinctual sense of trust. Instead of just speaking about logistics, we also spoke about relationships, culture, and family. It is because of you that I felt safe enough to start writing my story.

Amy, you have truly held me throughout this process. I have felt thoroughly seen, celebrated, and appreciated by you. Thank you for answering every question I have frantically asked, for being so patient and calm with me during my bouts of panic, and for advocating for me and rooting for my vision. I am convinced that you are my guardian angel, and I could not be happier that I completed this book in your loving hands.

Thank you to Somnath Bhatt, who collaborated with me on the illustrations in the book. Our collaboration was so effortless because you instantly knew the work that comes from my heart. I trusted you without any doubts, and we created something so special together. Thank you for sharing your intricate interpretations of love and freedom with me.

Immense appreciation to my beloved counselor, Aditi Bhattacharya, who taught me the sacredness of my continuance. You opened many portals in my heart and showed me compassion at times when I felt love was a myth. You challenged me with questions that I ask myself every day and you guided me through heartbreak, queerness, and confusion, and toward enlightenment.

I completed this book in Meanjin (otherwise known as Brisbane in Australia) and am deeply grateful for the friends who have supported my journey as a writer long before I even knew how to name it. It has been so wonderful returning home to you. Thank you to Elton Cheng, Rachel Cheng, Rayson Cheng, Tristram Jenkins, Josephine Nguyen, Connie Li, Caitlin Low (thank you for asking me to do my first reading ever!), Jeremiah Joseph, Paul Bao, Owen Gibson, Xavier Butler, Hamish McDonald, Anh Nguyen, Elena Dimeski, Gina Mattock, Raja Arden, Mary Harm, Lisa Nguyen, Lisa Chen, Simon Dang, Evi Papadopoulou, Adam Greer, Taj Poudel, and Zach La Haye.

I am grateful for all the writers who have opened and nourished my mind. Thank you for the ways that you have asked me not just to look deep within but also to critically engage with the world around me. I am constantly called to investigate the shadows and bask in the mutable unknown. I'm so lucky to have a community of writers who have guided me in New York City, namely, Alexander Chee, Fariha Róisín, Arabelle Sicardi, Neema Githere, Zeba Blay, Yrsa Daley-Ward, Alice Sparkly Kat, Mitchell Kuga, Andrew Nguyen, Jenna Wortham, and Adam J. Kurtz. I could not be the writer I am today if I did not read and listen to the wise gifts of my literary mentors, peers, and idols.

I am deeply indebted to Black feminist writers and Buddhists who have paved the way for most liberatory writing about love, healing, and transformation. I am especially grateful for Audre Lorde and bell hooks, two writers who completely radicalized me and shifted my perspective on our relationships with one another and the state. They are both literary ancestors who now watch over us with their guiding lights, and it is because of their generous offerings that I have been able to write my own stories as my response to their life's work.

I am grateful for the sacred land that I wrote this book on. I spent most of my time writing as a settler on unceded Lenapehoking and Tongva land on Turtle Island. I am deeply grateful for the Native communities of these lands and the Indigenous wisdoms I have learned through interconnected relationships. I completed this book in sacred Meanjin, the sacred country where I was born, and I am humbled by the wisdoms of the land and its honorable Aboriginal people. It is imperative and essential to work toward Indigenous sovereignty and land back.

And, finally, thank you to my ancestors, for bringing me into being and guiding me into this sacred existence. One day, I will be an ancestor too.

Resources

This section includes nonexhaustive lists of resources that I hope will be helpful to anyone who needs them. If you go to **mimizhu .net/resources**, you will find links to all the resources mentioned below.

There may be some valuable resources that I missed when I created these lists, and many of them are in the New York area. However, I will continuously update the link on my website to include additional locations and resources, in the United States and internationally.

HOTLINES

Anti-Violence Project: 212-714-1141
Call Blackline: 800-604-5841
Crisis Text Line: text "HOME" to 741741
National Domestic Violence Hotline: 800-799-SAFE
   (800-799-7233)
National Sexual Assault Hotline: 800-656-HOPE (4673)
NYC Well: 888-NYC-WELL
Safe Horizon:
   800-621-HOPE (domestic violence hotline)
   212-227-3000 (rape and sexual assault hotline)
   866-604-5350 (all hotlines)
Trans Lifeline: 877-565-8860

You can also head to the Don't Call the Police website (dontcall thepolice.com), which has many resources according to different needs in various cities in the United States.

THERAPY AND COUNSELING

Anti-Violence Project
Asians for Mental Health
Ayana Therapy
Black Men Heal
Inclusive Therapists
Latinx Therapy
Loveland Foundation
National Queer and Trans Therapists of Color Network
NYC Well
Open Path Collective
South Asian Therapists
Therapy for Black Girls

RESOURCE GUIDES AND MUTUAL AID DIRECTORIES

BUFU Cloud 9 Mutual Aid
Don't Call the Police
Herbal Mutual Aid Network (HMAN)
NYC Community Fridges
Solace by Natalia Mantini
Studio Ānanda

GRASSROOTS COLLECTIVES AND COMMUNITY ORGANIZERS

BUFU
CAAAV NYC
Community Action Teams (CAT-911)

CORPUS NYC
Disability Justice Culture Club
For the Gworls
Guanábana NYC
The Okra Project
People's Programs
PFLAG NYC
Playground Coffee Shop
Public Assistants
Radical Love Consciousness
Red Canary Song
Sanctuary for Families
Seeding Sovereignty
Soar Over Hate
Survived + Punished
Weaving Our Paths

BOOKSTORES AND BOOK CLUBS TO SUPPORT

1418 Fulton
1804 Books
Bluestockings Cooperative
Eastwind Books of Berkeley
Eso Won Books
The Lit. Bar
Marcus Books
Mil Mundos Books
Noname Book Club
Playground Annex
Reparations Club
Venus Roots book club
Yu and Me Books

Recommended Reading

This section includes my recommendations for reading and listening. Some are mentioned in the book and some are not. They are all seminal works that I am deeply grateful for and inspired by.

BOOKS AND OTHER WRITINGS

Akomolafe, Bayo, *These Wilds Beyond Our Fences*
Butler, Octavia E., *Parable of the Sower*
Chee, Alexander, *How to Write an Autobiographical Novel*
Cheng, Anne Anlin, *Ornamentalism*
Davis, Angela Y., *Are Prisons Obsolete?*
Fern, Jessica, *Polysecure*
Gilmore, Ruth Wilson, *Golden Gulag*
Haines, Staci K., *The Politics of Trauma*
Hanh, Thich Nhat, *The Heart of the Buddha's Teaching*
Hanh, Thich Nhat, *Teachings on Love*
Hogan, Linda, *Dwellings*
hooks, bell, *All about Love*
hooks, bell, *Communion*
hooks, bell, *Killing Rage*
hooks, bell, *The Will to Change*
Kaba, Mariame, *We Do This 'Til We Free Us*
Kimmerer, Robin Wall, *Braiding Sweetgrass*
Lorde, Audre, *A Burst of Light*
Lorde, Audre, *Sister Outsider*
Ma, Ling, *Severance*

Machado, Carmen Maria, *In the Dream House*
Mingus, Mia, *Leaving Evidence* (blog)
Montgomery, Nick, and carla bergman, *Joyful Militancy*
Mohapatra, Mon, Leila Raven, Nnennaya Amuchie, Reina Sultan,
   K Agbebiyi, Sarah T. Hamid, Micah Herskind, Derecka Purnell,
   Eli Dru, Rachel Kuo, *#8toAbolition* (downloadable PDF)
Odell, Jenny, *How to Do Nothing*
Owens, Lama Rod, *Love and Rage*
Piepzna-Samarasinha, Leah Lakshmi, *Care Work*
Prechtel, Martín, *The Smell of Rain on Dust*
Róisín, Fariha, *Who Is Wellness For?*
Russell, Legacy, *Glitch Feminism*
Somé, Malidoma Patrice, *Ritual*
Thom, Kai Cheng, *I Hope We Choose Love*
Vuong, Ocean, *On Earth We're Briefly Gorgeous*
Wang, Jackie, *Carceral Capitalism*
Yunkaporta, Tyson, *Sand Talk*

PODCASTS

Emergence Magazine Podcast
Franco, Niki, *Getting to the Root of It with Venus Roots*
Hemphill, Prentis, *Finding Our Way*
Tippett, Krista, *On Being*
Young, Ayana, *For the Wild*